STARING IN TO THE DARKNESS

Russell Lynn Irby

Contents

Chapter 1

Getting Started: Understanding Demonic Infestation, Oppression, and Possession

Introduction to Spiritual Warfare

In the realm of spiritual warfare, understanding the nature and extent of demonic activity is crucial for anyone involved in deliverance ministry. The terms "demonic infestation," "oppression," and "possession" are often used interchangeably, but they refer to different levels and forms of demonic influence. Recognizing these distinctions is essential for effectively combating these forces and helping those who are suffering.

In my years of deliverance ministry, I've seen firsthand the different ways demons can manifest and torment individuals. However, I've also learned the importance of not jumping to conclusions, especially when mental health issues might be involved. Distinguishing between genuine demonic influence and psychological disorders is critical to providing the right kind of help.

This chapter aims to differentiate between demonic infestation, oppression, and possession, discuss the similarities and differences between these phenomena and certain mental health disorders, and highlight the importance of involving mental health professionals in cases of suspected demonic activity.

Demonic Infestation

Demonic infestation is the lowest level of demonic activity. It typically involves the presence of a demonic entity in a location, object, or sometimes even an animal. Infestation does not involve direct control or influence over a person but rather manifests through various disturbances in the environment.

Signs of demonic infestation can include:

- Unexplained noises, such as knocking, footsteps, or banging

- Strange odors, often foul or sulfuric in nature

- Objects moving on their own or disappearing and reappearing in different places

- Electrical disturbances, such as lights flickering or electronics malfunctioning

- Cold spots or sudden drops in temperature

Infestation can occur in homes, buildings, or outdoor locations. It is often associated with places where occult practices have taken place, or where traumatic or violent events have occurred. This is why people who did nothing wrong can end up with demonic attachments and were the victims of an attack or incident. The demonic entity attaches itself to the location or person, often feeding off the negative energy present.

The goal of demonic infestation is usually to create fear and confusion. By causing disturbances in the environment, the demon aims to weaken the spiritual defenses of those present, making them more susceptible to further demonic influence.

Demonic Oppression

Demonic oppression is a more severe form of demonic activity that involves direct interference in a person's life. Unlike infestation, which affects a location, oppression targets an individual, causing physical, emotional, and spiritual distress.

Signs of demonic oppression can include:

- Unexplained physical ailments, such as headaches, nausea, or pain, with no medical explanation

- Sudden changes in mood or personality, including feelings of anger, depression, or anxiety

- Intrusive thoughts or voices that encourage self-harm or harm to others

- A sense of being watched or followed, often accompanied by feelings of fear or paranoia

- Unexplained accidents or a string of bad luck

Oppression can occur when a person has opened themselves up to demonic influence, either knowingly or unknowingly. This can happen through involvement in occult practices, sinful behavior, or even through curses or generational sins. The demon's goal in oppression is to break down the individual's will, isolate them from others, and ultimately gain more control over their life.

While oppression can be severe and debilitating, it is important to note that the person is not fully possessed. They still have free will and the ability to seek help and resist the demon's influence. This is the most common attack that has been encountered in my years of ministry. Infestation is often low key enough that people rarely seek help as it is often just passed off to life in general. Where the final stage, which is demonic possession, is so rare, I have only encountered a few times in over twenty years.

Demonic Possession

Demonic possession is the most severe form of demonic activity. In cases of possession, a demon takes full control of a person's body, often suppressing their consciousness and will. The demon speaks and acts through the person, often displaying knowledge, abilities, or behaviors that the individual would not normally have.

Signs of demonic possession can include:

- A complete change in personality or behavior, often becoming violent or aggressive

- Speaking in languages unknown to the person (glossolalia)

- Displaying superhuman strength or endurance

- Knowledge of hidden or distant events that the person could not have known

- An aversion to religious or blessed objects or prayers, often resulting in violent reactions

Possession typically occurs when a person has been subjected to severe oppression for a prolonged period, or when they have willingly invited the demon into their life. It is often the result of deep involvement in occult practices or extreme spiritual vulnerability. One of my earliest encounters with the demonic was a lady who liked her helper. She was abused by her husband, but since her helper had showed up, the husband was afraid of her.

During possession, the person is unable to control their actions and may have little or no memory of what occurs while the demon is in control. The demon's goal in possession is complete domination of the individual's body and soul, often leading to self-destructive or violent behavior.

Similarities and Differences Between Demonic Activity and Mental Health Disorders

One of the most challenging aspects of deliverance ministry is differentiating between genuine demonic activity and mental health disorders that may present with similar symptoms. Certain psychological conditions can mimic the signs of demonic influence, leading to confusion and misdiagnosis. Considering a demon will want to stay hidden in most cases, they will afflict those with mental disorders, thus having what would be seen as supernatural influence simply brushed off as effects of the disorder.

Mental Health Disorders That Can Mimic Demonic Activity

Some mental health disorders that can present with symptoms similar to demonic activity include:

1. **Schizophrenia**: This disorder is characterized by hallucinations, delusions, and disorganized thinking. Individuals may hear voices, see things that aren't there, or believe they are being controlled by external forces. These symptoms can resemble demonic oppression or possession, especially when the person expresses fear or paranoia about unseen entities.

2. **Dissociative Identity Disorder (DID)**: Formerly known as multiple personality disorder, DID involves the presence of two or more distinct identities or personality states within a person. These identities may have their own names, behaviors, and memories, which can appear similar to the behavior of someone under demonic influence.

3. **Bipolar Disorder**: This mood disorder is characterized by extreme mood swings, including episodes of mania and depression. During manic episodes, individuals may exhibit erratic behavior, increased energy, and impulsivity, which can be mistaken for signs of demonic oppression or

possession.

4. **Post-Traumatic Stress Disorder (PTSD)**: Individuals with PTSD may experience flashbacks, nightmares, and severe anxiety. These symptoms can be triggered by traumatic memories and may resemble the behaviors of someone experiencing demonic oppression.

5. **Obsessive-Compulsive Disorder (OCD)**: OCD is characterized by intrusive thoughts and compulsive behaviors. Some individuals with OCD may have religious obsessions or fears of demonic possession, leading to behaviors that mimic demonic influence.

Differentiating Between Demonic Activity and Mental Health Disorders

While there are similarities between demonic activity and certain mental health disorders, there are also key differences that can help differentiate between the two:

1. **Response to Religious Intervention**: One of the most significant differences between demonic activity and mental health disorders is the response to religious intervention. Individuals experiencing genuine demonic influence often have a strong aversion to religious objects, prayers, or scripture. They may react violently or with extreme discomfort when exposed to these things. In contrast,

individuals with mental health disorders typically do not exhibit such specific aversions. A caveat here is that I had one case where the person did have a mental health disorder where they thought they were possessed by a demon and through psycho-somatic reaction would have the adverse reaction. This was debunked when they were unknowingly given a bottle of water to drink that had been blessed, yet had no reaction.

2. **Supernatural Abilities or Knowledge**: Demonic possession may involve displays of supernatural abilities or knowledge, such as speaking in unknown languages, demonstrating superhuman strength, or revealing hidden information. These phenomena are not typically associated with mental health disorders. Thus a case where a person started levitating was an automatic diagnosis of supernatural presence.

3. **Sudden Onset of Symptoms**: Demonic activity often involves a sudden and severe onset of symptoms, especially in cases of possession. Mental health disorders, on the other hand, tend to develop gradually over time, with symptoms worsening as the condition progresses.

4. **Lack of Medical Explanation**: In cases of genuine demonic influence, medical professionals are often unable to find a

physical or psychological explanation for the individual's symptoms. This is not always the case with mental health disorders, where there is often a diagnosable condition that can be treated with medication or therapy.

The Importance of Involving Mental Health Professionals

Given the similarities between demonic activity and mental health disorders, it is essential to involve mental health professionals in any investigation of suspected demonic influence. Misdiagnosing a psychological condition as demonic activity can lead to unnecessary suffering, neglect of appropriate treatment, and potential harm to the individual.

A Personal Story: Dr. James Keller

Sadly, because of the world we live in, James Keller is not the name of my friend. With the ignorance and bias that is prevalent in the medical field, he is not able to show his belief of involvement with demonic warfare for fear of losing his well-earned position. I have always believed in the importance of a multidisciplinary approach when dealing with cases of suspected demonic influence. One of my closest friends, Dr. James Keller, is a psychologist who specializes in trauma and dissociative disorders. James and I have worked together on numerous cases over the years, and his expertise has been invaluable in helping me differentiate between genuine demonic activity and psychological conditions.

When James and I first met, he was skeptical of my work. He had spent years in the field of psychology, treating patients with a wide range of mental health issues, and he had seen how easily people could be misled by superstition and fear. He believed that most cases of supposed demonic activity could be explained by psychological factors and was hesitant to accept the idea of actual demonic influence.

Our partnership began when I encountered a particularly challenging case involving a young woman named Emily. Emily had been exhibiting signs of demonic possession, including speaking in strange languages, displaying unnatural strength, and having a violent aversion to religious objects. Her family was desperate for help, but I wanted to ensure that we were dealing with a genuine case of possession and not a psychological condition.

I reached out to James, asking for his professional opinion. He agreed to meet with Emily, albeit reluctantly, and perform a psychological evaluation. As James spoke with Emily, he quickly realized that there was something different about her case. Her symptoms didn't fit the typical profile of any known mental health disorder, and her reactions to religious objects were unlike anything he had ever seen.

In this instance, when I placed my hand on Emily's arm with my St. Benedict ring, which was also covered in blessed oil, there was an immediate reaction: she jerked back from me and, for an instant, looked hostile.

During one of our sessions, James witnessed something that would forever change his perspective. As I placed my hand on her head began to pray over Emily, she let out a scream as if in pain, her head jerking back from my touch. A foul smell filled the air. James unconsciously drew back when Emily looked him directly in the eyes and smiled. He would later tell me that he immediately had a feeling in his stomach as if it had been filled with ice and he was momentarily overwhelmed with a fight or flight feeling. Those of us in the field recognize this of when a demon is present. It is the primordial feeling of being in the room with a predator. She then began speaking in a deep, raspy voice.

"Get away from her!" the voice snarled, glaring at me with a hatred that sent chills down my spine. "She belongs to us!"

James froze, his disbelief evident on his face. He had seen people in the throes of psychosis, but this was different. There was a tangible presence in the room, something dark and malevolent, and it was clear that Emily was not in control of her actions.

I continued to pray, commanding the demon to leave in the name of Jesus Christ. Emily convulsed, her body thrashing as if trying to break free from an invisible grip. James watched, his skepticism replaced by a mixture of fear and awe, as the demon fought back, its grip on Emily tightening.

"James," I said, my voice steady, "help me pray. She needs us."

Without hesitation, James joined me in prayer, his voice shaky but determined. As we prayed together, the demon let out a final, agonized scream before releasing its hold on Emily. She collapsed into my arms, exhausted but free.

James was visibly shaken by the experience. "I've never seen anything like that," he admitted later. "I always thought there was a psychological explanation for everything, but this…this was different."

From that day forward, James and I developed a deep friendship and partnership. He became an integral part of my deliverance ministry, helping to assess individuals and ensure that they received the appropriate care, whether it was spiritual or psychological.

Pastor Russ's Anti-Personality Disorder

During my ministry, I've also had to confront my own struggles with mental health. I was diagnosed with an antisocial-personality disorder (APD) during my time in the Army, which ultimately led to my honorable medical discharge. APD, often referred to as antisocial personality disorder, is characterized by a pervasive pattern of disregard for the rights of others, lack of empathy, and often impulsive or aggressive behavior.

Staring into the darkness

Looking back, I can see how the disorder affected my life in those early years. I struggled with forming meaningful relationships, often feeling disconnected from others and lacking the ability to empathize. My behavior could be erratic, driven by a need for control and a fear of vulnerability.

My four years at North Georgia College, the military college of Georgia, and performing on the National Champion precision drill team, the Blue Ridge Rifles, followed by the military—with its rigid structure and emphasis on discipline—provided a temporary refuge. But even there, my tendencies eventually led to conflict. I found myself struggling to conform to the expectations placed upon me; my impulsive nature often clashed with the demands of military life. It wasn't long before my superiors noticed my difficulties and ordered a psychological evaluation.

When I was diagnosed with APD, it felt like my world had been turned upside down. I was discharged from the Army, and for a while, I felt lost and alone, unsure of what my future would hold. This disorder affects approximately three percent of the population with over half and as many as eighty-four percent incarcerated. But in that darkness, I found faith.

God had a plan for me, even when I couldn't see it. Through my struggles, I learned the importance of humility, empathy, and the power of God's love. I began to understand that my disorder didn't define me, and that with God's help, I could overcome my challenges and find a new purpose in life.

As I entered ministry, I found that my experiences gave me a unique perspective. I understood what it felt like to be on the outside, to struggle with feelings of disconnection and anger. As someone who had suffered under demonic attack and what can be a devastating mental disorder, it allowed me to connect with those who were suffering, to offer them hope and guidance in their darkest moments.

My friendship with James also played a significant role in my healing. He helped me understand my disorder from a psychological perspective, offering insight and support as I worked to build healthier relationships and develop a deeper sense of empathy. His willingness to walk alongside me, despite his initial skepticism of my work, showed me the importance of partnership and the power of God's grace.

The Importance of a Multidisciplinary Approach

Incorporating mental health professionals into deliverance ministry is crucial for several reasons:

1. **Accurate Diagnosis**: Mental health professionals can help determine whether an individual is experiencing genuine demonic influence or a psychological condition. This ensures that the person receives the appropriate care and prevents misdiagnosis and potential harm.

2. **Comprehensive Care**: A multidisciplinary approach allows for comprehensive care that addresses both the spiritual and psychological needs of the individual. This can include therapy, medication, and deliverance, providing a holistic approach to healing.

3. **Credibility and Support**: Involving mental health professionals can lend credibility to deliverance ministry, helping to bridge the gap between spiritual and medical communities. It also provides support for ministers, offering them guidance and insight into complex cases.

4. **Ethical Responsibility**: As ministers, we have an ethical responsibility to ensure that individuals receive the best possible care. This means recognizing our limitations and collaborating with professionals who have expertise in areas outside our own.

A Collaborative Case

One of the most memorable cases that James and I worked on together involved a young man named Kyle. Kyle had been struggling with what appeared to be demonic oppression. He experienced severe mood swings, heard voices telling him to harm himself and others, and had a strong aversion to anything religious. Kyle's parents reached out to me, desperate for help. They believed that their son was under demonic attack and wanted me to perform a deliverance. However, I felt that it was important to involve James in the assessment process, given the nature of Kyle's symptoms.

James agreed to meet with Kyle and conduct a psychological evaluation. After spending several sessions with him, James diagnosed Kyle with schizoaffective disorder, a condition that combines symptoms of schizophrenia, such as hallucinations, with mood disorder symptoms, like depression or mania. Kyle was the gentleman who unknowingly drank the holy water without issue, thus it was his mental disorder that was convincing Kyle he was being attacked by the demonic when there were none present.

James recommended that Kyle begin a treatment plan that included medication and therapy. While Kyle's parents were initially disappointed, they agreed to follow James's advice. Over time, Kyle's symptoms improved significantly, and he was able to regain a sense of normalcy in his life.

However, James and I continued to monitor Kyle's progress, remaining open to the possibility that there could be a spiritual component to his struggles. As his treatment progressed, Kyle began to express an interest in faith, and we worked together to provide him with spiritual guidance and support.

Through this collaborative approach, we were able to provide Kyle with the comprehensive care he needed, addressing both his psychological and spiritual needs. It was a powerful reminder of the importance of partnership and the value of bringing together different perspectives and expertise.

Conclusion

Understanding the distinctions between demonic infestation, oppression, and possession is crucial for anyone involved in deliverance ministry. It allows us to provide the appropriate level of care and support for those who are suffering and ensures that we do not inadvertently cause harm by misdiagnosing a psychological condition as demonic activity.

The similarities between demonic activity and certain mental health disorders underscore the importance of a multidisciplinary approach, involving mental health professionals in the assessment and treatment process. By working together, we can offer comprehensive care that addresses both the spiritual and psychological needs of the individual, providing hope and healing in even the darkest of situations.

My friendship with Dr. James Keller and my own experiences with anti-personality disorder have taught me the value of humility, empathy, and collaboration. We all have our struggles, but by leaning on each other and trusting in God's love and grace, we can overcome any obstacle and find a path to healing and redemption.

Chapter 2

Deliverance Ministry: A Distinctive Approach to Spiritual Freedom

Introduction: Two Paths to Spiritual Liberation

As a deliverance minister with over two decades of experience, I have encountered many misconceptions and misunderstandings about the nature of deliverance and how it differs from the exorcism rites of the Catholic Church. While both seek to liberate individuals from demonic oppression and possession, the methods, theology, and follow-up care in these ministries differ significantly. It is essential to recognize these differences, not to create division but to provide clarity and understanding for those seeking freedom from spiritual bondage.

Many modern churches shy away from discussing spiritual warfare or the existence of demons altogether. In some congregations, there is a reluctance to acknowledge the reality of evil spirits, often resulting from a lack of understanding or fear of the unknown. It seems to me almost blasphemous how a pastor can preach on demons and how Jesus delivered people from their possession, yet then deny their existence or influence in the world. Jesus spoke more about demons (thirty times) than he spoke about angels (twenty times). However, as believers, we are called to confront these spiritual realities head-on, equipped with the power and authority given to us by Jesus Christ. In this chapter, I will explore the distinctive elements of deliverance ministry, its divergence from the Catholic exorcism rite, and the importance of ongoing spiritual support and follow-up care after demonic removal.

Understanding Deliverance Ministry

Deliverance ministry is a broad term that encompasses various practices and methodologies aimed at freeing individuals from the influence of evil spirits. Unlike the more formalized exorcism rites of the Catholic Church, deliverance ministry is often less ritualistic and more flexible, allowing for a tailored approach that can address the unique needs of each individual. In deliverance ministry, the focus is not solely on expelling demons but on a comprehensive healing process that addresses the root causes of demonic oppression and ensures the person's spiritual, emotional, and psychological well-being. This not to say that the Catholic Church abandons the person after the sessions, as they absolutely do not. The brave and holy men that perform on the front lines for the Catholic Church that I have met in my ministry are some of the best and most caring people you could hope to find. It is just that these experts are sent to an area for one task and then because of the amount of work needed and the scant number of performers are sent to the next victim.

One of the core principles of deliverance ministry is the belief that all believers have the authority to cast out demons in the name of Jesus Christ. This authority is rooted in passages such as Mark 16:17, where Jesus states, "And these signs will accompany those who believe: In my name they will drive out demons." Unlike the Catholic Church, which reserves the right to perform exorcisms for priests who have been specially trained and authorized, deliverance ministry often empowers laypeople to participate in the process of spiritual liberation. The rub is that the Christian church whether Catholic or Pentecostal has done an abysmal job of training warriors to perform such actions and chooses more often than not to put their heads in the sand and act like demons don't exist.

Deliverance ministry typically involves several key steps:

1. **Identification**: This involves discerning the presence of demonic influence, which may manifest in various forms such as physical symptoms, emotional disturbances, compulsive behaviors, or unexplained phenomena.

2. **Renunciation**: The individual seeking deliverance is encouraged to renounce any involvement in occult practices, sinful behaviors, or generational curses that may have opened doors to demonic oppression.

3. **Repentance**: Confession and repentance of sins are crucial for breaking the legal rights that demons may have over a

person. This step often involves personal prayer and counseling to address unresolved issues and wounds. This is often the hardest part of the ministry as some memories may have been so horrendous as they are repressed or even hidden within mental health issues.

4. **Command**: The deliverance minister or team will command the demons to leave in the name of Jesus Christ, invoking His authority and power over all evil spirits.

5. **Restoration**: After the demons have been cast out, it is vital to fill the individual's life with the presence of the Holy Spirit, encouraging spiritual disciplines such as prayer, Bible study, and fellowship to prevent re-entry of demonic forces.

The Catholic Exorcism Rite: A Sacramental Approach

The Catholic Church's approach to exorcism is fundamentally different from deliverance ministry in several ways. Exorcism in the Catholic tradition is considered a sacramental, a sacred rite that invokes God's grace to expel demons. The rite of exorcism is highly formalized and ritualistic, involving specific prayers, blessings, and invocations that have been standardized over centuries. Only priests who have been specifically trained and authorized by their bishops are permitted to perform exorcisms, and they must follow strict guidelines set forth by the Church.

The Catholic rite of exorcism is based on a theological framework that views demonic possession as an extraordinary occurrence, distinct from ordinary temptation or oppression by evil spirits. The Church recognizes several stages of demonic influence, ranging from ordinary temptation to full possession, and the rite of exorcism is reserved only for the most severe cases where a person's will is completely overpowered by demonic forces.

Key elements of the Catholic exorcism rite include:

1. **Liturgical Structure**: The rite follows a prescribed order of prayers, readings from Scripture, and invocations of the saints and angels. The priest repeatedly commands the demons to leave in the name of Jesus Christ, using specific formulas that have been handed down through tradition.

2. **Use of Sacramentals**: The exorcism rite often involves the use of holy water, blessed oil, crucifixes, and other sacramentals that are believed to convey God's grace and protection. These physical elements are seen as extensions of the Church's authority and a tangible manifestation of God's power.

3. **Discernment Process**: Before an exorcism can be performed, a thorough investigation is conducted to determine whether the symptoms are truly of demonic origin. This process often involves medical and psychological evaluations to rule out natural explanations

for the person's condition.

4. **Focus on the Authority of the Church**: The Catholic exorcism rite emphasizes the authority of the Church as the representative of Christ on earth. The priest acts as an agent of the Church, wielding the power and authority given by Christ to His apostles and their successors.

5. **Emphasis on Prayer and Fasting**: Exorcism in the Catholic Church is often accompanied by periods of prayer and fasting, both for the exorcist and for those seeking deliverance. This spiritual preparation is seen as essential for invoking God's protection and power.

Key Differences Between Deliverance Ministry and Catholic Exorcism

While both deliverance ministry and Catholic exorcism seek to free individuals from demonic oppression, their approaches and underlying theology differ significantly. Understanding these differences is crucial for anyone involved in spiritual warfare or seeking deliverance from demonic influences.

1. **Authority and Accessibility**: One of the most significant differences between deliverance ministry and Catholic exorcism is the issue of authority. In deliverance ministry, the authority to cast out demons is believed to be given to all believers, regardless of their position within the Church

hierarchy. This belief is based on passages like Mark 16:17 and Matthew 28:18-20, which emphasize the authority of Christ given to His followers. In contrast, the Catholic Church reserves the authority to perform exorcisms for ordained priests who have been specifically trained and authorized by their bishops.

2. **Ritual vs. Relational**: The Catholic exorcism rite is highly ritualized, following a prescribed liturgical structure that emphasizes the Church's authority and the power of sacramentals. Deliverance ministry, on the other hand, is often more relational and less formalized, focusing on the individual's personal relationship with God and the authority of Jesus Christ. While deliverance sessions may involve prayer, commands, and Scripture, they are generally more flexible and adaptive to the needs of the person seeking freedom. This is why a deliverance minister may also work with those in the hold of demonic infestation and oppression. While an exorcism may be done if there is a case of extreme oppression as it may meet all of the requirements, it is usually reserved for full possession.

3. **Theological Focus**: The Catholic Church views demonic possession as an extraordinary occurrence that requires a specific sacramental response. Deliverance ministry, however, often sees demonic oppression as a more common

experience that can affect believers and non-believers alike. This perspective leads to a greater emphasis on identifying and addressing the root causes of demonic influence, such as unresolved sin, trauma, or generational curses.

4. **Follow-Up Care**: One of the most critical differences between deliverance ministry and Catholic exorcism is the approach to follow-up care. In deliverance ministry, there is a strong emphasis on ongoing spiritual support and discipleship after demonic removal. This follow-up care is seen as essential for preventing re-entry of demons and ensuring the person's continued spiritual growth and healing. In contrast, the Catholic Church's focus is primarily on the exorcism itself, with less emphasis on long-term follow-up care. While the Church encourages ongoing participation in the sacraments and spiritual life, the structured support and discipleship often found in deliverance ministry may not be as readily available.

The Importance of Follow-Up Ministry in Deliverance

In deliverance ministry, the removal of demons is not seen as the end of the process but rather the beginning of a journey toward spiritual healing and wholeness. I have told more than one person, dealing with the demonic is the easiest part of the ministry as God does the heavy lifting. Healing the person who may or may not participate as they should is the hard part. Once a person has been set free from demonic oppression, it is vital to address the underlying issues that allowed the demons to enter in the first place. This often involves a comprehensive approach that includes spiritual counseling, inner healing, and discipleship.

1. **Spiritual Counseling**: After deliverance, individuals may need guidance and support to help them understand what happened and how to move forward. Spiritual counseling can provide a safe space for people to process their experiences, ask questions, and receive biblical teaching on spiritual warfare and the authority of Christ. This counseling often focuses on helping individuals identify and renounce any remaining strongholds or agreements with the enemy that may have opened doors to demonic influence and to avoid opening new ones.

2. **Inner Healing**: Many individuals who seek deliverance have experienced significant trauma, abuse, or emotional wounds that have left them vulnerable to demonic oppression. Inner healing involves addressing these wounds through prayer, forgiveness, and the power of the Holy Spirit. This process can be lengthy and requires a compassionate and sensitive approach, but it is essential for ensuring lasting freedom and preventing re-entry of demons. This is especially true for Satanic Ritual Abuse victims who

will almost always have mental health issues also.

3. **Discipleship**: Deliverance is not a one-time event but an ongoing process of sanctification and spiritual growth. Discipleship involves teaching individuals how to live a victorious Christian life, grounded in the truth of God's Word and the power of the Holy Spirit. This may include regular Bible study, prayer, worship, and fellowship with other believers. Discipleship also involves helping individuals develop a strong prayer life and spiritual disciplines that will protect them from future attacks and keep them rooted in their identity in Christ.

4. **Community Support**: One of the most valuable aspects of follow-up care in deliverance ministry is the support of a loving and understanding community. Many people who have experienced deliverance feel isolated or misunderstood, especially in churches that are reluctant to discuss spiritual warfare or the existence of demons. Being part of a community that acknowledges the reality of spiritual warfare and provides encouragement and support can make all the difference in a person's journey toward healing and wholeness.

The Modern Church's Reluctance to Address Spiritual Warfare

Despite the clear biblical mandate to confront and cast out demons, many modern churches are hesitant to discuss spiritual warfare or the reality of demonic influence. There are several reasons for this reluctance, ranging from theological differences to fear of the unknown.

1. **Theological Differences**: Some churches, particularly those with a more liberal or progressive theology, may downplay or outright deny the existence of demons and spiritual warfare. They may interpret biblical references to demonic possession as metaphorical or symbolic, rather than literal. This perspective often leads to a focus on social justice, psychological counseling, and other forms of support, rather than spiritual deliverance.

2. **Fear of the Unknown**: Spiritual warfare can be frightening and unsettling, especially for those who have never encountered it firsthand. The idea of demons and evil spirits can evoke fear and anxiety, leading some churches to avoid the topic altogether. This fear is often compounded by sensationalized portrayals of exorcism and deliverance in movies and media, which can create a distorted and exaggerated view of what these ministries involve.

3. **Lack of Training and Understanding**: Many pastors and church leaders have not received adequate training in spiritual warfare or deliverance ministry. As a pastor with

the Assembly of God, I can attest that ministers receive little to no teaching on dealing with the demonic. Without a solid understanding of the biblical basis for these ministries and the authority believers have in Christ, they may feel ill-equipped to address issues of demonic influence. This lack of training can lead to a reluctance to engage in deliverance ministry, even when faced with clear signs of demonic oppression.

4. **Concern for Reputation and Acceptance**: In a culture that increasingly values scientific explanations and psychological understanding, some churches may be concerned about being seen as superstitious or out of touch if they talk openly about demons and deliverance. This desire for acceptance and respectability can lead to a downplaying or avoidance of spiritual warfare, even when it is clearly needed.

The Consequences of Ignoring Spiritual Warfare

The reluctance of some churches to acknowledge or engage in spiritual warfare can have serious consequences for those who are struggling with demonic oppression. When the reality of evil spirits is ignored or denied, individuals who are suffering may not receive the help and support they need to find freedom and healing.

1. **Lack of Deliverance**: Without a willingness to confront

demonic oppression, individuals who are struggling with spiritual bondage may not receive the deliverance they desperately need. This can lead to prolonged suffering, as well as the potential for further spiritual, emotional, and physical harm. This can often lead to substance abuse to self-medicate which only acerbates the issue or even worse, turn to new age or occult practices to find a solution.

2. **Spiritual Isolation**: When churches refuse to address spiritual warfare, individuals who have experienced demonic oppression may feel isolated and misunderstood. They may be reluctant to share their experiences for fear of being judged or dismissed, leading to a sense of isolation and a lack of support.

3. **Missed Opportunities for Growth**: Engaging in spiritual warfare and deliverance ministry can be a powerful catalyst for spiritual growth and transformation. When churches avoid these ministries, they miss out on opportunities to help individuals grow in their faith, develop a deeper understanding of spiritual authority, and experience the transformative power of God's love and grace.

4. **Failure to Equip Believers**: The reluctance to discuss or engage in spiritual warfare can leave believers ill-equipped to recognize and resist the enemy's attacks. Without proper

teaching and training, individuals may be more vulnerable to demonic influence and less confident in their ability to stand firm in their faith. We encourage people to give their life to Christ which makes than an instant enemy to the demonic forces, yet don't equip them to defend themselves.

A Call to Action: Embracing the Fullness of Spiritual Ministry

As a deliverance minister, I have seen firsthand the transformative power of God's love and the authority of Jesus Christ to set captives free. I have also seen the devastating effects of ignoring or denying the reality of spiritual warfare. It is time for the modern Church to embrace the fullness of spiritual ministry, including deliverance and spiritual warfare.

1. **Educate and Equip**: Church leaders need to educate themselves and their congregations about the reality of spiritual warfare and the biblical basis for deliverance ministry. This includes teaching about the authority of believers, the nature of demonic oppression, and the importance of prayer and spiritual disciplines. By equipping believers with knowledge and understanding, churches can empower them to stand firm against the enemy's attacks and live victorious lives.

2. **Create Safe Spaces**: Churches should strive to create safe and supportive environments where individuals feel

comfortable sharing their experiences with demonic oppression and seeking help. This may involve offering confidential counseling, support groups, or prayer teams that specialize in deliverance ministry. By providing a safe space for individuals to seek help, churches can ensure that no one suffers in silence or feels isolated in their struggles.

3. **Encourage Prayer and Fasting**: Prayer and fasting are powerful spiritual disciplines that can help prepare individuals and congregations for spiritual warfare. Churches should encourage regular times of prayer and fasting, both individually and corporately, as a means of seeking God's protection and power. By prioritizing prayer and fasting, churches can cultivate a culture of spiritual preparedness and reliance on God's strength.

4. **Promote Ongoing Discipleship**: Deliverance is not a one-time event but an ongoing process of spiritual growth and transformation. Churches should prioritize ongoing discipleship and support for individuals who have experienced deliverance, helping them to develop a strong foundation in their faith and a deep relationship with God. This may involve regular Bible studies, mentorship programs, or accountability groups that provide encouragement and guidance.

5. **Acknowledge the Reality of Evil**: Finally, churches must acknowledge the reality of evil and the presence of demonic forces in the world. While it is important not to sensationalize or focus excessively on the enemy, it is equally important not to ignore or deny his existence. By acknowledging the reality of evil, churches can better equip their congregations to recognize and resist the enemy's attacks, standing firm in the authority of Jesus Christ.

Conclusion: The Power of Deliverance Ministry

Deliverance ministry is a vital part of the Church's mission to bring healing and freedom to those who are oppressed by the enemy. While it differs from the Catholic exorcism rite in its approach, theology, and emphasis on follow-up care, it shares the same goal of liberating individuals from the power of darkness. By embracing the fullness of spiritual ministry, including deliverance and spiritual warfare, the Church can fulfill its calling to set captives free and proclaim the victory of Jesus Christ over all evil.

As believers, we are called to be agents of God's love and power in a world that is often dark and broken. By stepping into the authority that Christ has given us and engaging in the ministry of deliverance, we can bring hope and healing to those who are suffering, shining the light of God's love into the darkest corners of our world. The battle is real, but so is the victory, and it is ours through Jesus Christ, our Lord and Savior.

Demons in the Criminal Justice World

In my years of ministry, I've seen demons operate in various ways, but their influence in the criminal justice system is one of the most complex and insidious. The intersection of human sin, institutional corruption, and demonic influence creates a fertile ground for evil forces to manipulate both the oppressed and those in power. It's a battlefield where justice and mercy must be wrestled from the hands of spiritual wickedness, often operating unnoticed behind the scenes.

This chapter will explore how demons influence the criminal justice world and how we, as deliverance ministers, can confront and combat their presence within it.

The Demonic Hierarchy and the Criminal Justice System

Demons operate under a well-structured hierarchy, much like organized crime syndicates. At the top are powerful fallen angels—principalities and powers—that influence entire regions, governments, and systems, including the criminal justice system. These higher-ranking demons are more strategic and work to shape the policies, laws, and corruption that filter down to the individual level.

Beneath them are lower-ranking demons that afflict individuals, both criminals and those who work within the system. Their aim is to perpetuate cycles of violence, injustice, addiction, and despair. Understanding this hierarchy is crucial because it helps us know where and how to target our prayers and interventions.

In the criminal justice system, demons seek to foster:

- **Corruption**: Demons of greed, power, and control infiltrate institutions, manipulating judges, officers, and officials to bend the law for personal gain. They create a system where justice can be bought and the innocent suffer.

- **Violence and Hatred**: Demons of violence prey on individuals already prone to anger, pushing them toward acts of brutality, murder, and revenge. In prisons, these demons stir up hostility between inmates, guards, and even families.

- **Addiction and Despair**: Many within the criminal justice system, from prisoners to law enforcement officers, suffer from substance abuse or psychological distress. Demons of addiction and despair feed off this vulnerability, making it hard for individuals to break free from their chains—spiritual or physical.

- **Oppression and Injustice**: Demons thrive where systems perpetuate oppression. In criminal justice, this manifests in wrongful imprisonments, police brutality, racial discrimination, and systemic inequality. The oppressed are often targeted by demons to keep them locked in cycles of sin, addiction, and violence.

Demons and Criminal Behavior

Demons often target individuals already vulnerable to criminal behavior, exacerbating their sins and pushing them further into darkness. Many criminals I've encountered in my deliverance work were influenced by specific demonic spirits that exploited their weaknesses. These individuals may not have started out as hardened criminals, but demonic influence gradually took hold, driving them to commit acts of theft, murder, or abuse.

1. **Spirits of Violence and Revenge**: These demons thrive in environments of pain, poverty, and broken homes. They often latch onto individuals who feel abandoned or wronged, pushing them to commit acts of violence as a form of control or revenge. The most notorious serial killers, gang leaders, and violent criminals frequently report hearing voices or feeling compelled to act out horrific deeds, many of which are attributed to demonic influence.

2. **Spirits of Greed and Corruption**: Corruption is rampant in both the criminal world and the justice system itself. Demons of greed twist individuals' desires for power and wealth, leading them to manipulate the law or engage in criminal enterprises. Judges accepting bribes, officers planting

evidence, and criminals running illegal operations from behind bars are examples of how these demons operate.

3. **Spirits of Addiction**: Drugs, alcohol, and other substances are gateways for demonic influence. Addicts often feel trapped in an endless cycle of shame and destruction. Demons use addiction to weaken individuals, making them more susceptible to other forms of spiritual and emotional manipulation. Many crimes, from petty theft to murder, are committed by individuals under the influence of demonic spirits that fuel their addictions.

4. **Spirits of Lust and Perversion**: Sex crimes, trafficking, and abuse are often influenced by spirits of lust. These demons exploit the brokenness of individuals, driving them toward perverse acts that cause immense harm to others. In prison, these spirits thrive, preying on the most vulnerable and feeding off the pain and exploitation of both victims and perpetrators.

Demonic Influence in Prisons

Prisons are often hotbeds for demonic activity. The combination of isolation, brokenness, and deep emotional wounds creates an environment where demons can thrive. Many inmates are not just serving time for crimes committed in the physical world but are also spiritually bound by demons that manipulate their actions and thoughts.

In my ministry, I've worked with prisoners who described feeling an evil presence in their cells, hearing voices commanding them to harm others, or experiencing uncontrollable rage and despair. These individuals are often tormented by demons who feed off their past sins and guilt, deepening their spiritual bondage.

Even correctional officers and staff are not immune. Many face significant psychological and emotional tolls from working in such environments, often resulting in substance abuse, depression, or corruption. Demonic forces use these vulnerabilities to widen their influence, creating an atmosphere of fear, distrust, and violence.

How to Deal with Demonic Influence in the Criminal Justice System

1. **Prayer and Fasting**: Just as Jesus taught his disciples that certain kinds of demons only come out through prayer and fasting (Matthew 17:21), this is a vital tool in confronting the spiritual strongholds within the criminal justice system. For those of us working in deliverance ministry, sustained prayer and periods of fasting are essential in weakening the grip that demons have on both individuals and institutions.

2. **Deliverance Ministry in Prisons**: Bringing deliverance ministry into prisons can have a transformative effect on inmates. This includes prayer sessions, Bible studies, and

spiritual counseling aimed at breaking the chains of demonic oppression. Many inmates are open to deliverance because they recognize the forces of darkness in their lives and are desperate for freedom.

3. **Spiritual Discernment**: One of the most critical tools for working within the criminal justice system is discernment. Demons are master deceivers, and it requires the Holy Spirit's guidance to detect their presence, especially in complex cases involving mental illness, trauma, or addiction. Not every case of criminal behavior is caused by demonic activity, but spiritual discernment helps determine when and where demonic forces are at work.

4. **Establishing Christian Mentorship Programs**: Criminal justice reform requires both spiritual and practical solutions. Christian mentorship programs can provide prisoners with accountability, counseling, and biblical guidance. These programs help inmates identify demonic influences in their lives and offer them a pathway to spiritual and emotional healing. Once inmates are out of prison, these mentorships can continue to offer support as they re-enter society.

5. **Breaking Generational Curses**: Many inmates are caught in generational cycles of crime, poverty, and addiction. These patterns are often tied to spiritual strongholds passed

down through family lines. Deliverance ministers need to address these generational curses and pray for individuals to be freed from the sins and demonic influences that have plagued their families for generations.

6. **Engaging Law Enforcement in Spiritual Warfare**: Those working in law enforcement need spiritual support and protection. Deliverance ministry can equip officers and justice workers with the tools they need to combat not only physical crime but also the spiritual forces behind much of the violence and corruption they encounter. By teaching them how to pray, discern demonic activity, and guard their hearts against the temptations of power and corruption, we can protect those on the front lines.

A Case Study: David's Deliverance

One of the most powerful experiences I had was with an inmate named David, who had been incarcerated for multiple violent offenses. David had grown up in a home filled with violence, substance abuse, and occult practices. By the time he was in his twenties, he had already committed several crimes and was deeply entrenched in gang life. He felt trapped, not just by the prison bars, but by the darkness that seemed to follow him everywhere.

When I first met David, he told me about the nightly terrors he experienced. He would wake up paralyzed, feeling an unseen force pinning him down. He heard voices, mocking him, telling him to take his own life. He had tried to turn to the prison chaplain for help, but nothing seemed to work.

I prayed for David, commanding the spirits of violence, despair, and death to leave him in the name of Jesus Christ. As we prayed, David collapsed into tears, releasing years of guilt, fear, and anger. Over the next few weeks, he began attending Bible studies, and his demeanor changed. The anger in his eyes was replaced with peace, and he no longer experienced the demonic attacks that had plagued him.

David's transformation became a testimony to the other inmates, many of whom began seeking deliverance and healing. His story is a reminder that no matter how far someone has fallen into sin and darkness, the power of Christ can set them free.

Conclusion: Confronting the Darkness

The criminal justice system is a battleground not just for legal matters but for spiritual ones. Demons exploit every crack in the system—whether it's a corrupt judge, a desperate addict, or a prison guard teetering on the edge of despair. But with the power of prayer, discernment, and the authority given to us in Christ, we can confront and defeat these forces.

As deliverance ministers, we must remember that our battle is not against flesh and blood but against the spiritual forces of evil

(Ephesians 6:12). The criminal justice world may seem overwhelmed by darkness at times, but the light of Christ is always stronger. Our mission is to bring that light to the most broken, the most lost, and the most oppressed—and to show them that freedom is possible in Jesus Christ.

Chapter 3

The Burden of the Past

Introduction to Susan's Life

Let me tell you about a woman named Susan. Susan was the kind of person who could light up a room with her smile. She had a successful career, a cozy home, and friends who adored her. She was active in her community and her church, always willing to lend a hand or offer a word of encouragement. But behind that warm exterior, Susan carried a heavy secret that had been gnawing at her soul for over twenty years.

When Susan was just a teenager, scared and alone, she made a decision that would haunt her for the rest of her life—she had an abortion. It was a decision made in fear, in a moment of panic and confusion. She was young, unprepared, and terrified of what her future would hold with a child. She thought it was the best thing to do at the time, a way to keep her life on track. But almost immediately after the procedure, Susan felt a deep, overwhelming sense of regret and loss.

She never told anyone about the abortion, burying the pain deep inside, hoping it would go away. But as the years passed, that pain only grew. It festered like an untreated wound, a constant reminder of the choice she made. Susan threw herself into work, into church, into anything that might distract her from the guilt and shame that was slowly consuming her. But nothing worked. The guilt was like a shadow that followed her everywhere, whispering in her ear that she was unworthy, that she was a murderer, and that she could never be forgiven. She grew to hate herself, which in the world of spiritual warfare opens doors to darkness and would lead to a problem in her spiritual walk.

As Susan continued to struggle with her secret, she became more and more isolated. She stopped going out with friends, stopped enjoying the things she used to love, and was keeping her family at a distance. She was always on edge and always looking over her shoulder with a feeling that someone was watching her. There seemed to be a constant voice in her head that even her last place of refuge, her church where she taught Children's Church, would find out what she had done and remove her for what she did. She felt like a fraud, like she was living a lie, and the weight of that lie was crushing her.

It wasn't long before Susan's physical health began to deteriorate as well. She developed chronic headaches, insomnia, and a persistent ache in her chest that no doctor could explain. She was constantly tired, but she could never sleep, her mind racing with thoughts of what could have been, what should have been. She was haunted by visions of a child she would never know, a child she had chosen to end.

Staring into the darkness

And soon, that shadow began to take on a life of its own.

First Signs of Demonic Activity

It started with nightmares. At first, they were just fragments, flashes of dark, faceless figures that would disappear the moment she woke up. But as time went on, they became more vivid, more terrifying. Susan would wake up in a cold sweat, heart racing, after dreaming of shadowy figures surrounding her, accusing her, condemning her. "Murderer," they would whisper. "You can't escape what you did. You are the worst type of hypocrite; you try to help raise other children, but don't allow your own the chance."

These weren't just dreams; they were something darker, something that seemed to reach out from beyond the veil. She would see the shadowy figures in her peripheral vision, just out of sight, moving and whispering, taunting her with her past. They would appear in the corners of her bedroom, behind the curtains, in the mirror. They were always there, watching, waiting. Sometimes it would be a flashing shadow that would race from under her dresser to under her bed, but nothing would be there when she looked.

Then, the strange occurrences began. At first, it was just a feeling—a cold chill that would sweep through her house, even in the heat of summer. She would feel an icy breath on the back of her neck, a sensation of being watched, of being followed. The phone would ring three times and then stop but no name would be on the caller

ID, the temperature would drop, and a heavy sense of dread would fill the air. Soon after, it escalated. Susan started hearing noises in her home: whispers that seemed to come from nowhere, footsteps when no one else was around, doors creaking open on their own. The air in her house became thick, heavy with a sense of dread. She would hear her name being called in the middle of the night, a faint, almost inaudible whisper that would send chills down her spine.

One night, Susan woke to find her bedroom filled with shadows, darker than the night itself. The shadows seemed to move, to twist and writhe as if they were alive. Susan felt a presence in the room, something malevolent, something that was feeding on her fear and guilt. She tried to pray, but the words stuck in her throat, choked out by the overwhelming terror that gripped her heart. Not being able to pray, she felt the only protection she may have had abandoned her. She could feel the darkness closing in around her, suffocating her, pressing down on her chest like a heavy weight. She gasped for air, tears streaming down her face, but there was no escape. The shadows seemed to reach out for her, wrapping around her like a cold, clammy blanket. She felt like she was drowning, and like she was being pulled into the depths of a dark, bottomless abyss.

Escalation of Attacks

As the days turned into weeks, the attacks grew more violent. Susan would wake up with scratches on her arms, and bruises forming in the shape of hands as if someone or something had grabbed her in the night. The scratches were always three parallel lines, deep and painful, often drawing blood. She would find herself covered in bruises and welts, her skin black and blue from the relentless assault.

The whispers in her home grew louder, more insistent. "You belong to us," they would hiss. "You can never be forgiven. Heaven has no place for a killer of children. You chose your god Molech, and he will receive you soon." The voices would follow her wherever she went, echoing in her ears, filling her mind with darkness. She couldn't escape them, couldn't shut them out. They were always there, always taunting her, always reminding her of her past. She would fall on her knees, praying for forgiveness, thinking that would stop the attacks, but nothing seemed to work.

The nightmares became more vivid, more terrifying. Susan would dream of being dragged into a pit, surrounded by demonic faces that laughed and jeered at her, pulling her down into darkness. The pit was deep and endless, a swirling vortex of shadows and flames. She could feel the heat of the fire, the searing pain of the flames licking her skin. The demons would claw at her, tearing at her flesh, their eyes burning with hatred. Then the soul crushing vision of her unborn child was there, screaming at her "You condemned me to Hell. How could you hate me so much?" She would wake up screaming, the echoes of those hideous laughs still ringing in her ears. Her sheets would be soaked with sweat, her body trembling with fear. She would look in the mirror and see the dark circles under her eyes, the hollow look of someone who hadn't slept in days. She felt like she was losing her mind and slipping into madness.

Susan's friends and family finally noticed the change in her. She had become withdrawn, distant, and a shadow of her former self. She had stopped going to church because she felt like such a hypocrite teaching children about God when she was such an abomination. She had long since stopped seeing her friends and stopped doing the things she used to love. She was consumed by the darkness, by the guilt and shame that had taken over her life. She felt like she was living in a nightmare that was a never-ending cycle of fear and despair.

Desperate, Susan finally reached out to her pastor, hoping for some kind of relief. She confessed her past, every painful detail, and asked for help. The pastor listened patiently, offering words of comfort and encouragement. He prayed for her, asking God to lift the burden from her heart and bring her peace. Instead of peace, things only got worse. While the pastor prayed, Susan felt something cold and clammy wrap around her throat, squeezing, cutting off her air. She gasped, pulling away, her eyes wide with terror. The pastor, clearly shaken, told her she needed more specialized help. He told her that this was not something he had ever dealt with and was never trained to deal with. He called his old Bible professor, Dr. Wilmington, at Liberty University asking what he should do. Dr. Wilmington suggested she see a deliverance minister, someone who could help her break free from the demonic forces that had taken hold of her life.

That's when Susan came to me.

Seeking Deliverance

When Susan walked into my office, I could see the fear in her eyes. She was a woman at the end of her rope, desperate for some kind of peace. As she told me her story, I could sense the darkness that had latched onto her, feeding off the guilt and shame she had carried for so long. Her voice trembled as she spoke, her hands shaking as she recounted the nightmares, the attacks, the relentless torment she had been living with.

"Susan," I said, "we're dealing with something powerful here. These demons have taken root in your life, and they're not going to leave without a fight. But you need to know, God's power is greater than anything they can throw at you. The power of the Holy Spirit can drive them out, but you have to trust in Him completely."

The minute Susan walked in, the Holy Spirit awakened my discernment that we were dealing with a "murder" demon. I knew it would not go easy, just as I had told her, but it would leave if I could convince her to trust in God and in who she was in His Kingdom.

Susan nodded, tears streaming down her face. "I just want it to stop," she whispered. "I can't take it anymore. I feel like I'm losing my mind. I don't know what to do."

"God is always willing to help you, Susan," I assured her. "But you need to be ready for a battle. These demons won't leave easily, and they'll do everything they can to hold onto you. But with God's help, we can drive them out. Getting the demons out is the easiest thing that we are going to do, because God does all the heavy lifting. When we give Him the permission to go in and clean house, He will. The hard part is preparing ourselves to receive His love and walking in His grace from then on."

We began the first deliverance session that day. As I began to pray, the air in the room grew thick, almost suffocating. Susan's breath came in short gasps as she clutched the arms of the chair, her knuckles white. I could feel the presence of the demonic forces in the room, lurking, waiting to strike.

I prayed, "In the name of the Most High God, His Son, our Lord Jesus, and the wondrous Holy Spirit, I demand that any unclean spirit be bound. In Jesus's Holy Name, I demand, as a son of the Living God, in His Word, that anything bound in heaven is bound on earth. I bind any unclean spirit so that you will not be able to harm either myself or Susan. You will subjugate yourself to the name that is above all names Jesus."

Susan had claimed to be a Christian and thus should be a child of

Staring into the darkness

God. Like so many, she had allowed Satan to put her in fear and to believe that she was no longer saved. I had her say the sinner's prayer with me, and she was able, though very uncomfortable. No one under active possession can pray the name of Jesus, stating He is the Son of the Living God. This alerted me to the fact that, though she may be under strong demonic oppression, she was not completely possessed.

Shadows stretched across the walls. Something was getting in the way, and I had not received any notification from the Holy Spirit about what that might be. Susan was crying, as if her heart was breaking, and she tried to stand up as if to rush out. I demanded she remain seated in Jesus's name. From this, I received a look of sheer anger that still gives me chills years later as I write this. Whatever was present within her hated her and wanted her dead, but at that moment, it hated me even more.

I made a symbol of the cross on her forehead with holy oil. She seemed to shrink back in discomfort, but not in pain.

But finally, they seemed to weaken. The shadows receded, the room grew still, and Susan mentally and spiritually exhausted, looked on the edge of collapse. She told me that something was gone and that she had felt it leave. This was not anything new and I knew if my spirit that this was not the end. There was something Susan was still holding on to that was stopping Jesus from cleaning house. In many cases, the "Strongman" spirit will cast out others to give a sense of freedom and success only to attack even stronger later to try to crush the spirit. I could feel the hatred still was there, yet I felt it was as far as we were going to get that day. I encouraged her to follow up with her pastor and attend every service possible. I gave her praise music to play when at home, prayers to pray, and verses to read. She confessed that she prayed all the time, but it felt like God was not there. I almost cried at the look of pure abandonment on her face. I assured her that God is always there and waits on us with open arms.

Climactic Battle

But we weren't done. The demons had been pushed back, but they weren't gone. Susan called me that night and told me that as she was getting in the shower, a voice spoke to her telling her that "that cocksucker is weak, and he'll never remove us. Him and his God could not get us out. There is no hope". I told her not to be afraid as that is what they fed on. I reminded her, that this big bad spirit hid like a child today when it could confront. It knew it was hanging on by a thread and was scared and would do its best to frighten her into no longer pursuing her deliverance.

At the next session, as soon as we began to pray, the atmosphere in the room changed. The shadows returned, more powerful than before. The demons spoke, their voices filled with hatred. "She's ours!" they demanded in a coarse half yell. "You can't save her!"

Staring into the darkness

The room filled with a dark, oppressive energy, the air so thick it was hard to breathe. The shadows twisted and writhed, growing larger and more menacing with each passing second. They seemed to feed off Susan's fear, growing stronger and more aggressive as she trembled. We prayed with everything we had, invoking the name of Jesus, commanding the demons to leave. Then the lights flickered, and a dark shadow lunged at Susan, wrapping itself around her like a vice. She gasped, her eyes rolling back in her head as the demon tried to take control.

I demanded they stop their games in Jesus's name. I bound them by voice and action. The noises and shadows stopped immediately, and it released Susan. I knew it was time to deal with the stronghold that was allowing the demons so much power.

"I bind you in the name of Jesus Christ!" I shouted again, stepping forward, placing my hand on Susan's head. The demonic presence in the room was aggressive and the hate was almost palpable. I asked Susan what she was holding back. She had confessed her sin of committing abortion and repented, but this murder demon still had a stronghold that would not allow the love of Jesus to push through. If there is one thing constant about the supernatural world, it's that its laws are even more solid than those of ours. Gravity is a weak theory compared to supernatural laws and the demonic are top level lawyers when it comes to their rights under supernatural law. Susan told me she was not holding back anything.

That's when the Holy Spirit opened my heart and spoke to me: "She will not forgive herself for what she did. She is holding on to her self-hate so strongly that I cannot move. It was like being hit with a spray of cold water when first stepping into the shower. God's Word is supreme, and even He must obey it. To be forgiven, we must forgive, and that includes ourselves. It is Satan's dirtiest play that he convinces us we are not worthy of being forgiven, and by this, we stand in God's way of moving within us."

I asked Susan if she felt she could forgive herself for what she had done so long ago.

"No", she stated in a low defeated voice. "I will never be able to forgive myself for killing my baby".

I immediately yelled at her, "how dare you claim to love God and the children your care. How dare you sit here in the House of God and claim to have power greater than your creator."

Susan shrank back from my verbal attack. "I do love God and the kids. I've never believed I was more powerful than God."

I took her hands and now in a gentle voice, "God said He will forgive us anything if we only repent of it an ask. Don't you believe that, or is God just a liar?"

"I do believe he can forgive anything", she stammered. "He can't lie. He's God."

"Well, you just said you cannot forgive yourself because what you did was so bad. You must think you are better than God if you can do something He can't. Withholding forgiveness." I continued to hold her hands as I waited for my words to sink in.

I asked her, "Do you think your unborn child is at the feet of Jesus right now?". Tears flowed down her face as she nodded yes.

"Do you want to see your baby one day when you pass away? Do you want to hug then and tell them how much you love them? How sorry you are?" Again, she nodded while her chest heaved with sobs.

"Well, that's only going to happen if you allow yourself to forgive yourself".

She cried, "I don't know how".

I was crying as much as she was at the physical, emotional, and spiritual pain this child of God was going through now and had suffered for so long. My heart was breaking, but I knew the heart of Jesus was breaking even harder.

"Just say the words?" I said, smiling through my tears.

"It can't be that simple", she replied. "It just can't be that simple".

The demons seemed to sense that something was changing, and it fought with everything it had, lashing out at us, trying to break our concentration. The demons were furious because their stronghold was losing bricks. Wisdom and Word were dissolving the wall they had built. Their hold on Susan strong, but inwardly I continued to pray, calling on the power of Christ to drive them out. The battle raged on in the spiritual realm for this single soul. A young lady who was only one of billions on the planet, but the full armies of heaven would do battle for.

With the demons resisting at every turn, Susan looked up at me and said "I forgive myself" in the quietest voice as if she did not truly believe it. I told her to say it again.

She said it again, but stronger. Again, with more conviction. Susan convulsed in her chair, her body shaking. The air was thick with a palpable darkness, almost tangible in its intensity. It felt as though the room itself was alive with an unseen evil, pressing in on us from all sides. Yet she kept saying it and as she did she started to smile. The agony and the exhaustion seem to leave her face a little and you could see the beautiful child of God trying to shine through.

As I continued to pray and Susan claimed her victory, I could see the physical manifestations of the spiritual war we were waging. The demonic shadows seemed now almost physical in nature as they fought to reclaim that which they felt was theirs by right. There was an auditory hum in the room that was distracting and annoying.

I shouted above the chaos, "In the name of Jesus Christ, I command you to leave her! You have no power here!"

Susan's screamed, grabbing onto her lower abdomen where the child had been so many years ago, but for over a decade had housed something vile and dangerous. Multiple screams filled the room, a chilling sound that pierced through the darkness. Her eyes rolled back in her head; her face contorted in pain. I could see the shadows on the walls twisting and writhing, as if they were alive, mocking us, taunting us, but we did not relent.

"I rebuke you in Jesus's name!" I continued; my voice unwavering despite the fear that gnawed at the edges of my consciousness. I knew we were up against a formidable force, but I also knew that the power of Christ was greater than anything the demons could muster. "You no longer have any power here." She is a child of the living God and not yours to torment any longer."

I then prayed "Loving Jesus, have your warrior angels remove these unclean spirits and have them take them to your feet, to do with as you will. Your will be done as always.

Immediately, the tide began to turn. The shadows began to recede, the room gradually becoming less oppressive. Susan's breathing slowed, her body relaxed, and the pain in her abdomen left. The demons, sensing their defeat, let out a final, agonized scream before disappearing, leaving the room in an eerie silence.

Susan collapsed onto the table sobbing, her body shaking with relief and exhaustion. She was alive, and for the first time in years, she felt a glimmer of hope. But I knew we weren't done yet. The demons had been pushed back, but they weren't necessarily gone. In fact, this was the most dangerous time of deliverance: a clean house awaiting its new owner(s).

A Fragile Peace

Over the next few days, Susan began to experience a sense of peace she hadn't felt in years. The nightmares stopped, the whispers in her home ceased, and the oppressive atmosphere lifted. She felt lighter, as if a great weight had been lifted from her shoulders. For the first time in a long time, she could breathe without feeling like she was drowning in darkness.

She began attending church regular again and started spiritual counseling with her pastor. Finding solace in her faith and the support of her community helped with the healing process which would help keep the demons from returning. She reached out to friends she hadn't seen in months, rekindling relationships that had been strained by her isolation. She started sleeping through the night, waking up feeling rested and rejuvenated.

But despite the progress, Susan remained wary. She knew the demons weren't gone for good; they were simply waiting for an opportunity to return. She stayed vigilant, praying daily, reading her Bible, and surrounding herself with positive influences. She was determined to keep the darkness at bay, to reclaim her life and move forward.

Staring into the darkness

The Return of Darkness

A week later, the peace that Susan had found was shattered. She woke up in the middle of the night to find her bedroom filled with shadows once again, darker and more malevolent than before. The air was thick with an oppressive energy, and she could feel the weight of the demonic presence pressing down on her.

The whispers returned, louder and more insistent than ever. "You thought you could escape us?" they hissed. "You belong to us. You can never be free."

Panic set in as the shadows began to close in around her, wrapping around her like a suffocating blanket. She tried to pray, but the words stuck in her throat, her mind consumed by fear. The darkness was overwhelming, pressing in on all sides, crushing her under its weight.

Desperate, Susan reached for her phone and called me, her voice trembling with fear. "Russ, they're back," she whispered, her voice barely audible over the sound of her racing heartbeat. "I don't know what to do. Please help me."

I could hear the terror in her voice and knew we needed to act fast. I rushed to Susan's home, prepared for what I hoped would be a final, decisive battle.

The Climax of the Battle

The battle was on and everything was on the table. I went to get my keys and they were not in the drawer where I kept them. I went to get the spare set from out other care, but the doors locked when I went to open it. I prayed for the Holy Spirit to have the Holy Angels intervene and remove anything blocking me. The doors opened and I got my keys and left.

When I arrived, the house was in chaos. The shadows were everywhere, twisting and writhing on the walls, casting long, distorted shapes that seemed to stretch and bend unnaturally. The air was thick with a foul, sulfuric smell, and there was broken glass on the floor. Susan was in the living room, her body shaking with fear, her eyes wide and filled with terror. The demons had a strong hold on her, their presence palpable in the room. I immediately rebuked the spirits present in the name of Jesus and told Susan to pray with me. As soon as we began to pray, the atmosphere changed. The shadows grew darker, more solid, their forms taking on twisted, nightmarish shapes that loomed over Susan like malevolent giants. But we pressed on, refusing to be intimidated. We prayed with everything we had, invoking the name of Jesus, commanding the demons to leave. Susan gasped for breath, as the demon tried to take control. I stepped forward, placing my hand on Susan's head, my voice steady and firm. "We bind you in the name of Jesus Christ!" I shouted. "You have no power here, and you must leave this house now!"

Staring into the darkness

I reminded Susan who she was in Christ and the Word of God gave her authority over all unclean spirits. I told her to demand that the demon leave her house. It had no right there and was in the house of a Child of God. Remind them that she was the Temple of the Holy Spirit and they would never be allowed to defile that temple again. The demon let out a final, agonized scream and then was gone. The room fell silent, the shadows vanished, and Susan collapsed into my arms, sobbing, but free.

Aftermath and Healing

Many Christians who are attacked by demons have trouble believing in their rights as a child of God. We have full authority over unclean spirits, but it only works if we believe it. We must believe in the Word of God and use it as a sword in the world of the supernatural against evil beings who would destroy our soul. In the days and weeks that followed, Susan's life began to transform in ways she hadn't thought possible. The nightmares stopped completely, and the strange occurrences in her home ceased. The oppressive atmosphere that had once hung over her house like a dark cloud was replaced with a sense of peace and light. With the stronghold defeated, I blessed the house, and Susan dedicated it and the property to God as a Holy place. The fear that had once consumed her was gone, replaced by a renewed sense of hope and purpose.

Susan began to heal, both physically and spiritually. The bruises and scratches that had covered her body faded, leaving behind only faint scars. Her energy returned, and she felt stronger and more alive than she had in years. She threw herself into her faith, attending church regularly, reading her Bible, and praying daily. She found solace in the support of her community and her friends, who rallied around her, offering love and encouragement.

But the journey to healing wasn't easy. Susan still had to confront the memories of her past, the guilt and shame that had haunted her for so long. She began seeing a Christian counselor who helped her work through her emotions, helping her to understand that she was not defined by her past mistakes. She learned to forgive herself, to let go of the pain and the regret that had held her captive for so long.

She also began to share her story with others, speaking at church events and support groups, offering hope and encouragement to those who were struggling with their own burdens. She found a new purpose in life—helping others who were struggling with the same guilt and shame that had once consumed her. Her home, once a place of torment, became a sanctuary of peace and love.

Susan's transformation was nothing short of miraculous. She had gone from a woman consumed by darkness and despair to a beacon of light and hope. Her faith had been tested, but she had come out stronger on the other side, her relationship with God deepened and renewed.

The Ongoing Battle

But even as Susan found healing and peace, she knew the battle wasn't over. The demons that had once tormented her were gone, but they were not defeated. They were out there, waiting, watching, always looking for an opportunity to return. Susan remained vigilant, always aware of the darkness that lurked just beyond the light.

She continued to pray daily, to read her Bible, to surround herself with positive influences. She knew that she could never let her guard down, that she had to stay strong in her faith if she wanted to keep the darkness at bay. She also continued to work with her counselor, learning new ways to cope with the memories and the emotions that still lingered.

She became a fierce advocate for others who were struggling with their own demons, offering support and encouragement to those who felt lost and alone. She had asked about joining the ministry, but I told her that is something for God to decide. She is one of my first messages when I have a case as part of my prayer team.

Chapter 4

The Shadows of a Dark Past

Introduction to the Johnson Family

Now, let me tell you about Mark Johnson and his family. Mark had a past—one that he wasn't proud of. Before settling down and trying to build a new life, he was deep into the drug trade; immersed in a world filled with violence, crime, and sin. Mark had been one of the most feared men in his circle. He was known for his ruthless efficiency in handling "business," which often meant resorting to violence to protect his territory and his interests. His life in the gangs was expressed by the moto Laugh Now/ Cry Later which was emblazoned by a laughing and crying Mardi Gras mask tattooed on his left forearm.

He had done things that haunted him to this day. Acts of brutality that no one should ever have to carry on their conscience were as commonplace as choosing where to go for lunch. There were people he had beaten nearly to death, deals that had gone bad where he had to take matters into his own hands, and even a few men whose lives he had ended with his own hands or on his orders. Mark's past was a dark and twisted tapestry of violence and sin, painted in blood, fear, and greed. Then came the reckoning when he was arrested for drug possession with the intent to distribute. Five years spent at

Powhattan Prison just outside of Richmond, Virginia that changed his life. While there, he started attending services just to get out of his cell, but things he heard had an effect on him and led him to think that there was more to life than banging till dying.

While in lockup, he continued his education and earned his business degree. He attended services regularly, and though he enjoyed the time there and the people, he never bought into the whole "God loves you for you" business. He kept out of trouble, which at Powhatan was a job in itself, joined their culinary program, and was released after only three and a half years.

As part of his parole plan, he moved into a halfway house, stayed away from the drug business, and got a job at Sodexo, a company that embraces people who have made mistakes and want to change their lives.

Mark had managed to escape his past and thought he was done with that life but would find out it was not done with him. He worked hard, moved up and eventually became a chef. He married a wonderful woman, Lisa, who knew only a little of his past which included the drug possession charge, and together, they had two beautiful kids, Emily and Jacob. They moved to a quiet neighborhood, far from the chaos of his former life, hoping to start fresh. Mark found a solid career, made new friends, and tried his best to be a good husband and father.

But sometimes, the past doesn't let go so easily.

Initial Demonic Encounters

It started subtly, almost innocuously with strange noises at night, objects changing locations, cold spots in the house, etc. Mark tried to dismiss these things, telling himself it was just the wind or his imagination. But deep down, he knew better. He had been preyed on often when young but had later become an alpha predator on the streets and those instincts were going off, but for what reason he could not figure out.

One night, Mark woke up to the sound of footsteps in the hallway. Slow, deliberate, heavy footsteps that sent a chill down his spine. He grabbed the baseball bat he kept by the bed and left Lisa asleep as he crept toward the door with his heart pounding in his chest. It wasn't the first time his past had come to pay a price as he could not possess a gun with his felony past. The hallway was pitch black, but he could feel something watching him, something malevolent lurking in the shadows. This place of solace and security, of peace and joy where he enjoyed the warmth of love with his family, suddenly felt as dangerous as the cellblock at Powhattan or maybe worse. As he opened the door, the footsteps stopped. The hallway was empty, silent. Mark stood there, his grip tightening on the bat, straining to see into the darkness. He couldn't shake the feeling that something was there, just out of sight, watching him, waiting.

Staring into the darkness

He immediately went to the kids' room praying there was nothing there to hurt them. He slid open their door and could only see his angels sleeping peacefully. What should have given him great relief only caused his anxiety to grow as he could feel something was there; something that wanted to hurt him and his loved ones. He continued to walk around the house, looking for anything that wanted to cause harm. As he entered the living room, Spanks, the family pet who was a three-year-old Pitbull rescue was standing with his rear against the wall staring across the room as life looking directly at something. Spanks' tail was tucked all the way underneath, his head was lowered, and his ears laid all the way back. Mark stared as hard as he could at the area Spanks was looking at but could see nothing. Lamination from the outside lights came in through the windows, giving much better vision than the bedroom or hallway. There was no way something could be in the room and not be seen.

"Spanks", Mark called. "Spanks". The dog never broke his stance or acknowledged he heard anything. His eyes were focused, and he was frozen in place, as solid as a marble statue. Mark could hear what sounded like a combination of a low whine and growl emanating from Spanks' chest. Mark could feel the presence stronger than ever. It felt like his stomach was full of chunks of ice and his whole body was breaking out in a cold sweat. He had no idea how long they stood there, staring at nothing when suddenly as if waking from a dream, there was nothing. Spanks shot across the room to where he had been staring, looking every way and sniffing in confusion. Mark called him again, and this time Spanks came running over, seemingly overwhelmed with relief to be with Mark.

"That was some weird shit, huh boy", Mark grinned as he scratched the dog behind the ears. "Some real weird shit." After taking a moment to finish looking around with Spanks glued to his side, they found nothing out of place and no further feeling of malice.

"No more Tres Locos Taqueria for us before bed, huh", Marked grinned as he continued to pet Spanks. Spanks looked back at him but did not seem pleased in the least. Mark stopped smiling and agreed. "Yeah, you felt it too. I don't think that was just tacos talking, but I'm glad you're are here just the same."

Over the next few nights, the incident repeated itself, but grew worse. The kids began waking up in the middle of the night, screaming that someone was in their room and that when they woke up, they could see someone with a top hat standing at the foot of their bed, just watching them. They described feeling cold hands touching them, pulling at their sheets, whispering their names in the dark. Lisa would feel something cold brush past her, like a gust of icy wind, even when the windows were shut tight. And then there were the shadows—a dark, looming figure with the hat that seldom moved and seemed to just look at them until he would just disappear.

Staring into the darkness

Mark remembered his time at services from prison and tried to pray, tried to push back the fear that was growing in his heart, but every time he did, the feelings of danger and evil seemed to grow stronger, more aggressive. He could feel the darkness closing in around his family, suffocating them, feeding off their fear and it wasn't long before they were under constant attack.

The Dangers of the Past

As the attacks grew more intense, Mark began to realize that his past might be catching up with him. He had tried to leave his old life behind, but he knew that some things couldn't be so easily forgotten. He thought back to all the people he had hurt, all the lives he had destroyed in his pursuit of power and money. He remembered the faces of the men he had killed, the cold, lifeless eyes staring back at him as their blood pooled on the ground.

Mark had been a drug dealer, but he was more than just a businessman—he was an enforcer. When someone crossed him, they paid the price. He had broken bones, shattered jaws, and crushed skulls. He had taken lives with his own hands, feeling the life drain out of them as he choked them, stabbed them, or shot them point-blank. He had tortured people for information, leaving them broken and bloody, begging for mercy that never came. Just the thought of someone being a rat for the cops meant you and possible even your loved ones paid the price.

There was one incident that stood out above the rest, one that he could never forget. A member of his crew that he had grown up with; a person who had grown up in his same building and played with him at the playground. He had spent countless nights at this person's house, eating food in his house while watching cartoons, and called his mom "Auntie". Mark had received word that this guy was stealing from him. He had started using the merchandise and was skimming both product and cash. He was cutting the product to produce extra before selling to the customers who had started complaining. So, Mark took matters into his own hands. He cornered the guy, his boyhood friend, in an alleyway one night, his rage boiling over as he beat the man to within an inch of his life. He could still hear the sound of the man's bones cracking under his fists, the wet, gurgling sound of blood filling his lungs as he begged for his life. Mark had left him there, broken and bleeding, a message to anyone who dared steal him.

That was the life Mark had left behind. The life he had tried so hard to forget. But the darkness had a way of finding you, no matter how far you ran.

Escalation of Attacks

As Mark's fear grew, so did the intensity of the demonic attacks. The children would be thrown from their beds by invisible hands, screaming as they landed hard on the floor. Lisa would wake up with bruises and scratches on her body, marks that hadn't been there the night before. They were deep, jagged wounds, as if she had been clawed by something with long, sharp nails.

Mark was plagued by horrific nightmares where he found himself back in his old life, surrounded by the faces of those he had wronged, their eyes filled with hatred and pain. In these dreams, they accused him, cursed him, dragged him back into the darkness he had tried so hard to escape. He would wake up drenched in sweat, his heart pounding, the sound of their voices still echoing in his ears. Mark's mental health and very core of existence was off kilter. He was a survivor, a predator, an Alpha and yet he could not protect his family. His wife and children were suffering under attack, and he was powerless to stop any of it.

During the day, the atmosphere in the house was thick with tension. There were times when a dark shadow would seem to pass through the room. The walls would groan and creak as if the house itself was under strain. Objects would fly off shelves, lights would flicker uncontrollably, and the sense of dread became overwhelming. The worst was Spanks. He stopped eating and would just want to lay in his bed and whine as if in pain. Mark had taken him to the vet, but she couldn't find any physical problem. It crushed Mark's heart to see those loving, loyal eyes stare at him in pain, wanting help from his friend and master, but not receiving any.

One evening, as the family sat down for dinner, the power went out suddenly. The room plunged into darkness, but that wasn't the worst of it. The moment the lights went out, a deep, guttural growl echoed through the house, a sound that no earthly creature could make. The children screamed, Emily grabbed his arm in panic and Spanks let out the most hideous wail of a creature in great pain. Mark loosened Lisa's grip and grabbed a flashlight, desperately trying to find the source of the noise. But the beam of light only illuminated more darkness—shadows that seemed to move on their own, twisting and writhing in the corners of the room. Finally, it shone on Spanks, who was curled in a tight ball in his bed, head lifted wailing in pain.

Lisa was crying, clutching the children to her chest as Mark tried to calm them all down. But he knew, deep in his heart, that this was beyond his control. The past he had tried so hard to leave behind had come back to haunt him, and it wasn't just him suffering for it—his family was caught in the crossfire.

The attacks grew more personal, more targeted. That night, Mark woke up to find himself paralyzed, unable to open his eyes, move or speak. While he was trapped in darkness, he could feel a heavy weight on his chest, pressing down, squeezing the air from his lungs and he could feel an evil presence right beside him. He tried to scream, but no air would come out. He felt he would be okay if he could just scream and break loose from this hold. Then, he was able to make a low wheezing noise coming from is throat. He kept trying until he could feel things loosening within him. Tears poured down the side of his face and sweat broke out all over him as he strained against the evil invisible force holding him down. Finally, a scream burst from his lungs, his eyes flew open, and his body shook as if being released from bonds. Yet what he saw almost made him wish his eyes were glued shut gain. He could see a dark figure standing at the foot of his bed, its eyes glowing red in the darkness, a malevolent grin spreading across its face. It did not say anything for even move. It just stared at him as if it was a serpent and Mark was a mouse, paralyzed in fear and waiting to be devoured. When it finally spoke, the sound was low, growling voice, a voice that chilled him to the bone. "You can't escape us, Mark. We know who you are. We know what you've done, and you belong to us."

The figure leaned towards him, moving at a snail's pace, its hands reaching for his throat. The hands had not even touched him, yet he struggled to breathe. He wanted to fight back, but he was helpless. Out of the corner of his eye, he could see Lisa still sleeping on her side, turned away from him. How could she still be sleeping with everything going on? Mark could feel the icy fingers wrapping around his neck, squeezing tighter and tighter, choking the life out of him. Just as he was about to pass out, the figure vanished, and Mark was able to move again. He gasped for air, his body shaking with fear and adrenaline. As if released from a magic sleep only found in Disney movies, Lisa started awake. One look at Mark, and she burst into tears. Throwing her arms around the man she loved, she cried into his chest and through her sobs, "I can't do this anymore. We need help".

Mark knew he couldn't handle this on his own any longer. The fear that had once been a distant hum in the back of his mind was now a deafening roar, and it was tearing his family apart. Even with everything that had happened, the worst was yet to come. As he walked into the kitchen to get a glass of water, Mark passed Spanks laying in his bed. He leaned down to scratch behind his ears only to feel Spanks completely limp. As his head lolled over to the side, Spanks's right eye was open but was not seeing anything. Spanks was dead.

Mark collapsed to the floor, holding his dead friend. Tears burst from his eyes as he sobbed over Spanks' dead body. Another innocent body tallied to Mark's violent past. He just felt numb as he walked back to the bedroom and shared the new with Lisa who immediately started crying. The next morning, with no avenues left to turn, swallowing his pride, he reached out for help.

A Warning of Things to Come

Another time, I was in my gym playing with my ferrets between lifts when I felt a hand on my shoulder. I spun around, my arm lifting and hand curling into a fist to strike. Too many years working death row and isolation at Mecklenburg and Nottoway Correctional

Centers had formed that habit. I expected to see someone standing behind me, but there was no one there. I could feel it now, and I knew something was coming—something powerful and angry. The demons were trying to intimidate me and scare me off before I even knew what I would be facing.

I gathered my thoughts, took a deep breath, and began to pray, asking God for protection and guidance. I pled the blood of Jesus over myself, my family, and anything attached to my family. I prayed for supernatural protection from Heaven's Army and for the Holy Spirit to use my gift of discernment about what was coming. My spirit answered: murder. It's strange that many of my cases deal with past abortion, so I immediately assumed this was the same as the murder demon answer. Not only was I wrong in this, but I was about to start one of the most difficult cases of my life.

As I prayed, the oppressive feeling in the room began to lift, and the gym seemed to return to normal. Sam and Dean, the ferrets, were back in their box and had no desire to exit. Things may have returned to normal, but the message was clear: a battle was on the horizon.

Later that night, I received the call from Mark. His voice was desperate, shaking with fear and exhaustion. "I've tried everything," he said, his words tumbling out in a frantic rush. "But it's getting worse. I can't protect my family from this; it killed out dog Spanks. Please, help us." I immediately notified my prayer team that I had a case and that I would need them to start praying for me.

Arriving at the Johnson Home

Before arriving at the Johnson home, I prayed prayers of cleansing and protection. I prayed that whatever was present would not be able to attach to me or follow me after I leave. I had my Olive wood, St. Benedict blessed crucifix, my blessed salt, Holy Water, and blessed oil. The CZ 85 was tucked in a concealed holster behind my right hip. With my Bible and the faith in my Father, I took a first step into a world of madness. When I arrived at the Johnson home, I could feel the darkness before I even stepped out of the car. It was a heavy, oppressive feeling that made the hairs on the back of my neck stand up. Whatever was there was dark, evil, and full of hate. Having the gift of discernment is a wonderful gift, but when I am close to the demonic, it seems like just the opposite.

Mark greeted me at the door, his eyes hollow and red-rimmed. He looked like a man who had been to hell and back. His shoulders were hunched, and his movements were slow, as if every step was a struggle. Lisa stood behind him, clutching her arms around her body, her face pale and drawn.

Inside, the air was thick with tension, and they looked like they hadn't slept in days. The fear was etched into their faces, and it was clear that they were all at their breaking point. The house itself seemed to groan under the weight of the oppressive energy. It was like walking into a pressure chamber, each breath heavy and labored. The walls seemed to close in, the shadows stretching and reaching, as if alive.

I knew that this was a place where evil had taken root, and it wasn't going to leave without a fight—or possibly ever. I asked about the kids, and Mark responded that they had taken them to Lisa's parents' house, as I had asked, until this was over.

Mark led me to the living room, where we sat down and he began to tell me what he said was everything, but I would later find out was not true. He told me about drug dealing, and how he had tried to turn his life around. But the demons had latched onto that past, using it as a weapon against him. They were trying to drag him back into the darkness, and they were willing to destroy his family to do it. I knew he was lying while he spoke to me. There were parts of his past that he was not willing to share yet. As he spoke, I could see the pain and regret in his eyes. He had tried to leave his old life behind, but the demons, being legalistic as they are, were using it against him, feeding on his guilt and fear. They were determined to make him pay for his sins, to drag him back into the pit he had clawed his way out of.

The Battle Begins

I turned on my praise music CD and began to pray, asking God to cleanse the house and protect the family. I started my walking tour of the house and could feel the immense pressure and dark presence all over. During a typical case, most of the darkness seems to focus one or two places, but in Mark's house, it was all over as if a supernatural blanket had been thrown over the entire property. Yet the worst of all was in Mark's bedroom and the spot in the living room where Mark had said he and Spanks had felt something present. As I unpacked my bag and sat down to interview the Johnson's, I felt a poke in my lower left side. Ignoring this, I continued to get ready for the interview. That's when I felt a slap to the back of the head. Not immensely hard, just annoying and insulting.

"In the name of Jesus, I demand you stop. I bind you from hurting anyone present or attached to anyone here! You will bow your knee to the King of Kings and Lord of Lords. By his holy Word, I have authority over all spirits as a Child of the King, brought into sonship by the sacrifice of Jesus on the cross." I immediately felt another slap on the back of the head, which caused me to smile a little. I have been in battles for years and even with my experience and time in the trenches I sometimes forget that dealing with the demonic is a literal process. There are rules.

"You will cease to provoke or touch me in any way, in the name of Jesus". The pokes and slaps immediately stopped.

"You can't save them, preacher," the voice hissed, its tone filled with malice. "They belong to us". Startled, I looked by to Mark who was sitting at the table smiling at me. I knew immediately that it was not Mark who was looking at me or speaking to me. Emily's hand flew to her mouth, and she leapt to her feet and moved away from Mark to the other side of the table, as if the wooden item could block whatever sat there.

I stared at whatever was inhabiting Mark. "You don't get to choose who gets saved and who doesn't.

"And you do", it smiled.

"Nope, not me. I just get to decide what you will do here. And right now, in Jesus' name, you will be silent and let John speak to me again."

The demon retaliated violently. The walls shook, pictures fell from the walls, and the windows rattled as if a powerful wind was trying to break through. A dark, oppressive force coalesced in the room, and I could feel the weight of it pressing down, trying to crush my spirit, but I refused to back down.

I asked Lisa to sit back down. She approached her husband as if he was a cobra readying to strike. Finally, she sat down, but made no move to grab the offered hand. Mark looked like he had been slapped in the face when he saw the fear in Lisa's eyes as she looked at him. I don't think I can imagine the hurt that would hit my heart if my wife every looked at me that way, as if she was afraid to be in my very presence.

I asked Lisa if she was a Christian. She told me that she had gone to church with her family growing up but had not continued when she went to college. She had not been in a church since then except when she visited her mom and dad. Even then, it only happened when it was her and the kids. Whenever Mark traveled with her, he was always ill on Sunday's and never went. She had never thought about it until now. She said she guessed she was a Christian as she had attended a Christian church her whole life.

I smiled, "Going to church does not make you a Christian any more than going into a barn makes you a horse. Have you every prayed the sinner's prayer and offered your life and soul to our Lord and Savior, Jesus Christ?"

As I asked the questions, the demonic presence grew more aggressive. Shadows started to writhe and twist, forming grotesque shapes that loomed around us, as if threatening to engulf us in darkness. I could feel the demonic presence trying to seep into my mind, filling it with images of pornography, then violence and despair—images of Mark's past, the men he had hurt, the lives he had destroyed. They were trying to weaken me, to make me doubt myself, but I held firm, clinging to my faith like a lifeline.

"No", she said quietly. I then had her repeat after me, the most beautiful of prayers. The prayer that causes all of heaven to grow quiet. The pray of a lost soul asking Jesus into their heart and allowing the Holy Spirit to flood them with his presence. Lisa gave her soul to Christ. There were tears in her eyes when she opened them and looked at me.

"You are a daughter of the most high God now. You are a citizen of heaven, and these creatures no longer have authority over you".

"But I don't feel any different", she stated sheepishly.

I smiled, "That's because you are only looking at the natural and what just happened here is in the supernatural. Trust me when I tell you, There's a difference."

As I looked at Mark, I was suddenly reminded that the battle still raged on, with the demon throwing everything it had at us. The shadows seemed to grow arms and claws, reaching out to grab us, to pull us into the darkness. My head felt like it was full of cotton suddenly and I could not concentrate. It was in this moment that I made a mistake and I allowed it to distract me.

"I rebuke you in Jesus's name!" I shouted; my voice filled with authority. "You have no power here! You will not harm this family any longer!"

The demon howled in rage, the sound so loud it made my ears ring. The temperature dropped suddenly, and Mark winced as if someone had slapped him across the face. He suddenly looked like he as battling to stand. His face contorted he looked like he was choking. Then, the thing within laughed at me.

"You and your fake authority. You aren't in control here. We are. This one is mine and I'll do whatever I wish. Mark screamed in pain and Lisa jumped away from him and rushed over to my side. I told her not to worry as they could not hurt her".

"But what about Mark", she asked as he trembled in pain in his chair. I realized that this was not a case of demonic oppression, but that Mark was fully possessed, and it was only the bindings put on the demon from the beginning that kept the worst from happening.

"In Jesus's name I demand you allow Mark to speak gain. You will stay silent". The muscles in Mark's face strained in effort and then went slack. I could tell he was back. I then asked Mark if he could say the sinner's prayer with me. He started to speak, but then went silent. He seemed to strain with all his might but could not say the word Jesus. This further confirmed my suspicion of possession. The demon was not going to allow Mark to say the sinner's prayer. He was not going to let him say the beautiful name of Jesus.

I have spoken before about the legalistic world of spiritual warfare. The demonic are fully aware of their rights and can quote scripture better than any pastor you've seen. They know the Word of God better than most people know their own face. We had finally reached the lie. Standing between Mark and the freedom that Jesus brings was the stronghold he had allowed to remain by holding back his past.

"Mark. What have you not told be yet? There is something you have not admitted and repented for. What are you holding on to that won't allow the demon to let you go?"

It hurt my heart to see the look of desperation and loss in Mark's eyes. His eyes were glued to Lisa's.

"I can't", he cried staring at her.

"You can and you must", I answered. "There is no other way. There is nothing so horrible in your past that God cannot forgive you for. There is no darkness he cannot pull you from, but he can't do it if you don't repent for your past. Without repentance, there is no forgiveness. Jesus will not accept a partial surrender, and the demons will not give you up unless Jesus takes over."

"I'm not concerned with God's forgiveness. "I'm more worried about Lisa's". There it was. The stronghold the demon had built convinced Mark that he would lose Lisa and his family if his past was brought out. He was putting worldly things before spiritual things. He did not have faith in God or Lisa.

Lisa seemed to melt as she burst into tears. "There is nothing you can tell me that would make me stop loving you"

Mark's eyes were hollow and filled with tears. "You have no idea what I have done. You can't imagine in your worst nightmares what your husband is capable of".

"Then become a new man", I broke in. When you give your life to Christ, you are a new man. Born again through the sacrifice of our Lord and Savior. Also, if you don't then this will never end. How can you say you love your wife and children and still be willing to have them go through this? Do you love them enough to lose them, to keep them safe?"

"I would die for them", he cried.

"Then do that but do it in the spiritual realm. Give your life to Christ and let the old man die. Be reborn in a new life where the darkness will no longer own you, but you live in the light of God's grace. Help me, save them."

Mark closed his eyes and set his jaw. After a moment, he opened his eyes and nodded at me. Slowly he looked at Lisa and spoke.

"I'm a murderer. When I told you, I had been involved with drugs, that was not the end. I ran a drug crew and to do that meant violence. To do that meant killing anyone who stood in my way or screwed with my business. I've shot, stabbed, and even killed people with my bare hands. My drugs killed innocent people who never hurt me. I took their money and gave them poison."

While he spoke, Lisa started shaking her head back and forth as if she refused to believe what she was hearing and as long as she refused to believe it, there was no way it was real.

"Lisa, I don't even know how many people I've killed with that poison. I'm so sorry. I wish I could take it all back and be the man you thought you married. After I got out of prison and met you, I thought I left all of it behind. You were so wonderful and didn't treat me different just because I had been in prison. But I remember when we met, you said you didn't care if I had been involved in drugs, it's not as if I killed anyone. The look you had on your face then as you accepted me and was willing to love me. I could never admit to you what I had done and risk losing you. You were the only good thing that had ever happened in my life, and I could not stand the thought of you not being in my life."

"Mark", I asked taking his gaze back from Lisa. Are you sorry for what you did in your past? Do you repent of your past and are you willing to live your life for Jesus?"

"I cannot tell you how sorry I am. How sorry I am, that I am not the man my family thought I was. I wish on my life that I had never done those things."

"Mark", I implored as I grasped his hand. Repeat the sinner's prayer with me.

Tears flowed down his face anew. "What if I can't. I'm scared to try, because what if I can't and I'm lost forever. Even with what I said, it's not scratching the surface of the pain I caused."

"Maybe you can't, but God can. For you immortal soul; for Lisa; for your kids, will you try?"

Mark nodded again and this time as he attempted to speak the name, Jesus, it flowed like water off his lips. He immediately stopped as if he suddenly didn't know what to do. So great was the expectation that it would not happen, so great had the stronghold over his soul been created he was speechless when it broke. Then with renewed spirit, a smile and fresh flowing tears, he gave his life to Christ.

He immediately started heaving and retching.

"Grab a trashcan", I yelled at Lisa while jumping up and running over to Mark. His back hunched and he continued to give painful dry heaves with his body clenching so hard, he could not inhale breath. Lisa came running over with the kitchen trashcan and held it in front of him. Just when it seemed he was going to pass out with the strain, he retched up a foul-smelling black ichor. Imagine fish guts sitting out in the Texas heat for a week. During my time as an MP, I have seen dead bodies that sometime had gone undiscovered for weeks. That still sits at a second place over this smell. He kept retching over and over, puking out the mixture which was far more than he could have physically held in his stomach.

When it was done, he was physically drained. He collapsed back into his chair and almost toppled over. Only remaining sitting by

Lisa grabbing and supporting him. She wiped his hair back as she held his head to her chest and looked at me.

I shook my head, "We are not done yet".

The Turning Point

After what felt like hours of intense spiritual warfare, the demon's strength began to wane. It had released its hold on Mark, but it was far from defeated. What were once growls of threat turned to shrieks of rage and pain, and the oppression in the room began to recede, pulling back like a tide going out to sea. The oppressive force that had been pressing down on us started to lift, and the air grew lighter.

Mark was beside me, his face wet with tears, but there was a look of determination in his eyes. He was fighting for his family, for his soul, and he wasn't going to let the demons win. Lisa and held him to her chest, tears streaming down her faces as they whispered prayers of their own. They were scared, but they were strong, and their new faith was a beacon of light in the darkness. It's always amazed me how new converts can sometimes have faith a hundred times stronger than those who have been believer for decades.

"In the name of Jesus Christ, I command you one last time: Leave this house and never return! You will go to the feet of Jesus to do with you as he will. I call on the armies of Heaven under the authority of the Archangel Michael, to bind you and remove you from here where you no longer have a right to be." I shouted, feeling a surge of divine power flowing through me.

There was a final, blood-curdling scream as the demon was forced out. The house seemed to sigh one last time, and then, as suddenly as it had begun, everything went still. The lights stopped flickering, the air warmed, and the heavy atmosphere lifted, leaving the room feeling lighter, almost peaceful.

Mark collapsed to his knees, sobbing with relief. Lisa dropped with him, holding him close as they realized it was over. They were exhausted, emotionally and physically drained, but they were alive—and they were free.

Rebuilding and Redemption

Over the next few days, the Johnson family began to rebuild their lives. The house was blessed and the land was pledged to the most high God. It was no longer a place of fear and torment, but a sanctuary of peace and love. The oppressive darkness that had once filled every corner was gone, replaced by a warm, inviting light that seemed to fill the house with a sense of hope and renewal.

Mark made a vow to God that he would never allow the darkness of his past to control him again. He began attending church regularly, becoming more involved in the community, and dedicating his life to serving others. He wanted to make amends for the wrongs he had done, to help those who were struggling with the same demons that had once plagued him.

Staring into the darkness

He started working with at-risk youth, sharing his story, and warning them about the dangers of the life he had once lived. He became a mentor, a role model, someone they could look up to and trust. He knew he couldn't change the past, but he could make a difference in the future, and that was enough for him.

Lisa, too, found solace in her faith, becoming active in the church much to the delight of her parents and finding comfort in the support of their friends and community. The children, Emily and Jacob, slowly began to heal, the fear that had once gripped them fading with time and love. They were a family again, stronger and closer than ever.

The scars of the past would always be there, but they were no longer a source of torment. Mark had found redemption through the power of Christ, and with it, the strength to protect his family from any further spiritual harm. The Johnson home, once a place of darkness, had become a beacon of light, a testament to the power of faith and the victory of good over evil.

A Final Encounter

Several weeks after the deliverance, I received a call from Mark. He sounded calm, but there was a note of urgency in his voice. "Russ, there's something I need to tell you," he said.

When I arrived at the Johnson home, Mark met me at the door, with a serious look on his face. "I think you should come to the basement," he said.

We made our way down the stairs, and as we reached the bottom, Mark pointed to a spot in the corner. "I was cleaning up down here a few days ago, trying to get rid of some old stuff, when I found this," he said, holding up a small, weathered box.

I took the box from him, feeling a strange energy emanating from it. It was old and worn, the wood cracked and splintered, but there was something about it that felt…off.

"I had forgotten it was here," Mark continued.

I nodded, opening the box carefully. Inside, I found a collection of strange items— a card of St Muerte, a small, carved figurine, and a piece of parchment smeared with blood. There were also small photos like out of a yearbook.

As I examined the contents of the box, I felt a chill run down my spine. I could sense a dark energy coming from the items, a residual evil that seemed to cling to them like a shadow. This was no ordinary box—it was a tool of dark magic, a conduit for demonic forces.

"I had that box when I was a dealer. St Muerte was out patron saint. That blood is from my first victim and the pictures are of some of the ones I killed." I want it gone, but did not want to just throw it in the trash.

"You did the right thing, Mark," I said, carefully closing the box. "These items are definitely connected to the attacks, because they are connected to your past life.

Mark's face paled, and he swallowed hard. "What do we do?"

"I'll destroy it," I said firmly. "These items have no power on their own, but they've been used for evil purposes and represent evil actions. We need to break their connection to you, to finally cleanse this house once and for all."

I took the box to a church of a pastor friend of mine. I prayed over the items, asking God to break their power and remove any remaining darkness. Then, one by one, we threw them into the fire I built in a burn pit, watching as the flames consumed them, reducing them to ashes.

As the last of the items burned, I shoveled dirt over the ashes. Confining them to holy ground forever. The darkness was gone, the last remnants of the demonic presence that had haunted the Johnson family finally destroyed.

Conclusion

The Johnson family's journey was a long and difficult one, but in the end, they found the peace and redemption they had been searching for. They learned that no matter how dark the past may be, there is always hope for a brighter future. They found strength in their faith, in each other, and in the love and support of their community.

For me, being a part of their journey was a humbling experience. I witnessed the power of God's grace and mercy, the strength of the human spirit, and the victory of light over darkness. The battle had been fierce, but in the end, the Johnson family was finally free.

Their story is a testament to the power of faith, the importance of redemption, and the unyielding strength of the human soul. It serves as a reminder that no matter how far we may fall, there is always a way back to the light. All we need to do is have faith, reach out for help, and trust in God's love and grace to guide us home.

Chapter 5

The Dark Invitation

Introduction to the Hargroves

In my many years as a deliverance minister, I've witnessed countless tales of spiritual warfare, but few have left as deep an impression as the case of the Hargrove family. What began as a seemingly harmless evening of entertainment spiraled into a nightmare that threatened to tear their family apart.

Tom and Pam Hargrove were a young couple who had recently settled into a quiet, suburban neighborhood. They were the epitome of the perfect family, well-liked by their neighbors and known for their warm hospitality. Their home was often filled with laughter and the sounds of friendly gatherings. One evening, they decided to host a small get-together, inviting a few close friends for a night of wine, finger foods, and good company.

The evening started out like any other, filled with music, chatter, and the cheerful clinking of glasses. But as the night wore on, and the alcohol began to flow more freely, someone suggested they add a little excitement to the mix by bringing out an Ouija board. It was supposed to be a fun, spooky game, a lighthearted way to end the night on a thrill. Tom and Pam, like many others, viewed the Ouija board as nothing more than a novelty—an amusing, albeit eerie, parlor game. So, they went along with the idea, setting up the board in the middle of their living room, surrounded by candles to create a fitting atmosphere.

The group gathered around, hands resting on the planchette, and began to ask questions. At first, it was all fun and games, with laughter filling the room as they tried to move the planchette themselves, pretending it was being guided by some unseen force.

But soon, the atmosphere shifted. The planchette started to move on its own, slowly spelling out words that made the room fall silent with awe.

At first, everyone thought it was a trick, a prank played by one of the friends to scare the others. But as the answers became more direct, more personal, the mood in the room grew tense. They asked for a name, and the board spelled out "Kimmy." There was a palpable silence as everyone exchanged uneasy glances, wondering if they had indeed made contact with a real spirit.

Sally, one of the guests, pressed on, asking for more details about Kimmy. The planchette moved again, spelling out that Kimmy was a six-year-old girl who had died in a fire at a Catholic school in 1958. She claimed to be one of ninety-two children who had perished that day. Intrigued and a bit frightened, Sally's husband quickly pulled out his phone and searched online for any record of such an event. To everyone's shock, he discovered that on December 1, 1958, a fire had indeed broken out at Our Lady of Angels School in Chicago, killing ninety-two children and several nuns.

The group was stunned, their previous skepticism replaced by a mix of fear and fascination. They continued to communicate with Kimmy, who described her loneliness, her sadness, and her longing for her parents and friends. Pam, feeling a maternal instinct for the lost little girl who was the same age as her own daughter Jessica, felt her heart ache. When Kimmy asked if she could come back to visit, Pam, moved by sympathy, said, "Anytime you want." Little did she know that by uttering those words, she had just given full rights for "Kimmy" to take up residence in her home.

First Signs of Demonic Activity

After that night, strange things began happening in the Hargrove household. At first, it was subtle with a cold spot here, an unexplained noise there, or an object mysteriously out of place. Tom dismissed these occurrences as mere coincidences or the lingering effects of their spooky game. Pam, however, couldn't shake the feeling that something was terribly wrong.

Their daughter Jessica was the first to show signs that something more sinister was at play. Jessica had always been a bright and imaginative child, often hosting tea parties for her stuffed animals and talking to her imaginary friends. After that fateful evening, her tea parties began to take on a much darker tone. She started talking to a new "friend" named Miss K, who she insisted was real.

At first, Pam thought it was just Jessica's vivid imagination at work. She even found it endearing how her daughter seemed to care so much for her new invisible friend. But as the weeks went by, Jessica's behavior grew increasingly strange. She became more withdrawn, often staring off into space as if listening to someone only she could hear. Her once joyful laughter was replaced by an eerie silence, and her playful demeanor turned cold and distant. Then came the violent outbursts. Jessica would scream and cry for no apparent reason, thrashing about as if she were being tormented by something unseen. She started saying strange things, like "Miss K doesn't like you, Mommy," or "Miss K says Daddy is bad." Pam's concern grew into fear as she watched her sweet little girl transform into someone she barely recognized.

Escalation of Attacks

One night, Pam heard Jessica talking in her room long after she was supposed to be asleep. When Pam opened the door, she found Jessica sitting in the dark, her eyes wide and unblinking, whispering to a figure she called Miss K. Pam, her heart racing, asked Jessica what she was doing. Jessica turned to her, her voice unnervingly calm and distant. "Miss K. says you're going to die, Mommy. He says I have to help him."

Fear gripped Pam's heart as she realized that this was no imaginary friend—this was something far more dangerous. She tried to comfort Jessica, but the little girl just smiled, a chilling, unnatural smile that sent shivers down Pam's spine.

From that moment on, the attacks on Pam began in earnest. It started with small things—bruises that appeared on her arms and legs without explanation, objects falling from shelves and narrowly missing her head, doors slamming shut on their own. Tom, ever the skeptic, suggested logical explanations for these occurrences, but Pam knew better. She could feel the malice in the air, the invisible eyes watching her every move.

One evening, as Pam was cooking dinner, she felt a sharp pain in her side, as if something had hit her. She gasped, dropping the knife she was holding, and when she raised her shirt and looked down, she saw deep scratches on her skin, as if claws had raked across her flesh. She knew she hadn't done it to herself—something unseen had attacked her.

Later that night, as she lay in bed, Pam was jolted awake by the feeling of hands around her throat, choking the air from her lungs. She thrashed and struggled, but she could not see anyone. Specks of darkness started to explode in her vision, and her head felt like it would burst from pressure.

When it seemed like she was done for, she finally managed to break free, gasping for breath. Tom woke to find her shaking, terrified beyond words.

Seeking Help

The next morning, Pam and Tom knew they needed help. Desperate for answers and fearing for their lives, they went to their local parish, hoping that the church could offer them some sort of guidance or relief. The priest listened to their story with concern but ultimately told them that it was beyond his expertise, and he referred them to the diocese, where they met with a Catholic bishop. The bishop listened to their plea but remained skeptical. He explained that exorcisms were rare and that the church approached them with caution. Without concrete evidence of demonic possession, he couldn't authorize an exorcism. Pam and Tom left the meeting feeling hopeless, unsure of where to turn next. The Church had always been a constant in their lives. Jessica had been baptized by the priest who suddenly was of no spiritual help.

That's when they found me. Their priest knew of a husband-and-wife team of Benedictines who did investigations for the Catholic church when the bishop allowed. He contacted them, explaining that he felt something was amiss but that the diocese was not convinced there was enough. They told him that they knew of a deliverance minister and recommended they give me a call. When Pam contacted me, I could hear the desperation in her voice. She told me about the strange occurrences, and the attacks on her and her daughter. As part of the investigation, I asked if they had been in contact with any occult practices and that's when Pam told me about the Ouija board session. They only hit the high points and did not tell me everything said. I had no idea that they had unknowingly invited a demon acting as a familiar spirit into their home, and it wasn't going to leave without a fight. They had basically just given a demon, squatters rights to their home and family.

Ignorant of the entire situation, I had both admit and repent of their use of the Ouija board and participating in occult practices. Once this was completed and they renewed their faith in Christ Jesus, I thought we had all we needed to do battle, but I was very wrong.

The Battle Intensifies

When I arrived at the Hargrove home, I could feel the oppressive atmosphere the moment I stepped through the door. Oh, the joys of discernment! It's like being a perfumer or sometimes a nose whose olfactory senses are so acute they are ensconced in the middle of a trash dump. Someone with the gift of discernment is already sensitive to the supernatural, so getting to a place where there is a powerful presence can be almost overwhelming.

The air was thick with a presence—something dark and malevolent that had taken root in their lives. Tom and Pam looked exhausted, worn down by fear and sleepless nights. But it was Jessica who worried me the most. The little girl sat in the corner of the room, her eyes wide and hollow, whispering to someone only she could see.

I started with prayer, asking God to protect us and cleanse the house of any unclean spirits. As I began to pray, Jessica's behavior changed instantly. Normally, I try to have children not be present during a deliverance unless necessary and since she seemed to be the focal target, it absolutely was. Jessica started to scream, a high-pitched wail that echoed through the house, her small body writhing on the floor as if in pain. The lights flickered, and a cold wind swept through the room, even though all the windows were closed.

"Miss K says you can't stop her!" Jessica shouted, her voice layered with something darker, something not her own. It was clear that the demon had a strong hold on her, using her as a vessel to spread fear and chaos. The game never changes as the playbook is as old as time. Even the human pawns of evil in the middle east today use children as shields to protect themselves from attack. It started on the supernatural realm earlier than recorded time. The parents looked helpless as they witnessed their beautiful princess being assaulted by something evil and couldn't do anything to stop it.

As I continued to pray, the demon retaliated with full force. The room shook, pictures flew off the walls, and furniture slid across the floor as if being pushed by an invisible hand. Then a foul odor filled the air—the stench of decay and death.

I prayed to the Holy Spirit within me to tell me why this demon was here and how it could be defeated. Typically, the situation did not escalate to Defcon 5 from the beginning unless I had done something to harass the demon or put it in fear of being cast out. This told me that somehow, this demon was unsure of its hold and probably was not high in the hierarchy of Hell. It was literally like lashing out in an immature stomping of its foot when it thinks its toy is going to be taken away.

I stepped forward, holding my crucifix out like some poor movie adaptation, and commanded the demon to leave in the name of Jesus Christ. "You have no power here," I said, my voice firm despite the fear gnawing at the edges of my mind. "By the blood of Christ, I bind you and cast you out!"

The demon shrieked, a sound so inhuman that it sent chills down my spine. Jessica convulsed on the floor, her body arching in unnatural ways as the demon fought to maintain control. But we pressed on, praying with all the strength we had, refusing to back down.

The demon lashed out at Pam, who suddenly screamed and fell to the ground, clutching her side as fresh scratches appeared on her skin. I rushed to her side, continuing to pray, while Tom tried to comfort their daughter, who was now thrashing and screaming as if she was having a grand mal seizure.

A Battle of Wills

"I have the right to be here! You have no right to send me away!"

the demon screamed from Jessica's poor body.

"What did any of you say Kimmy", I asked suddenly. Pam and Tom looked at me like I had lost my mind.

"I don't understand", Pam shot back. "What's that got to do with anything?"

The Holy Spirit was rolling out knowledge to me like fresh baked Krispy Kremes and I was swallowing as fast as I could.

"Just answer my question. Kimmy is Miss K. What did you say to Kimmy?".

Revelation seemed to wash over Pam as she stared at me.

"Kimmy asked if she could visit, and I told her anytime. It's my fault this thing is attacking us", she sobbed.

As the spiritual battle waged on, the demon employed every trick to break our resolve. Objects in the room began to levitate and then fly across the space with violent force. Glasses shattered against walls, and chairs were hurled across the room as if by an invisible giant. The walls themselves seemed to pulse with a dark energy, a palpable malevolence that filled the air with a sense of dread. Jessica's screams grew louder, blending with guttural growls and hissing that seemed to emanate from her small frame. Her voice, no longer her own, echoed with the ancient malice of the demon that sought to consume her. The sound was a chilling mix of her innocent child's voice and something far older, far more sinister.

Pam, despite her fear and the fresh wounds on her skin, found the strength to join me in prayer. Together, we called upon the name of Jesus, invoking His power and authority over all darkness. Tom, holding his daughter tightly, began to pray as well, his voice shaky but growing stronger with each word.

Grabbing Pam by the forearm, I said, "You as the homeowner gave the demon the right to live in your home and you have the right to evict it. This is a Christian household, and it has no right to be here.

"By the authority given to us through Christ," I shouted, "we command you, foul spirit, to leave this child and this house! You have no place here!"

The room seemed to resist my words, as if the very structure of the house was holding its breath, waiting to see if we would falter. But we did not. We continued to pray, louder and with more conviction, pushing back against the darkness that had dared to invade this home.

A Relentless Assault

The demon's retaliation was immediate. As I spoke the name of Jesus, a force pushed against me trying to distract me and break my concentration. For a moment, I felt as if the air I was breathing had thickened like a Mississippi summer day after an afternoon thunderstorm and my eyes burned with pain from the smell of sulfur. I closed my eyes, refocused on my connection with the Holy Spirit and the promises of authority from the Holy Word and resettled myself, refusing to let the demon see my fear.

Pam and Tom, witnessing the attack on me, redoubled their prayers, their voices rising above the chaos. Jessica, though no longer thrashing and screaming, seemed caught in a battle between the light and the darkness within her. Her small body trembled violently, her eyes rolling back into her head as the demon fought to maintain its grip.

Suddenly, the temperature in the room plummeted even further, and a thick, black mist began to seep from the corners, swirling around us like a living thing. It seemed to sap the very strength from our bodies. But still, we did not stop. In fact, I had been doing this long enough to know that the attacks always intensified when the end was near. The demon was holding on by its fingernails and was trying anything to back us off.

"Jesus, help us," I cried out, my voice barely audible over the cacophony of noise and the oppressive weight of the mist. "We need Your strength, Your power, Your protection. Have your warrior angels remove this abomination from this house of Christ."

As if in response, a sense of well-being seemed to fill my soul, pushing out the negativity and oppression. Looking at Pam, I could see she was feeling it too. The Holy Spirit was filling us with a renewed sense of strength and courage.

The Power of Prayer

I continued to pray, shouting over the noise, my voice filled with the authority given to me by Christ. "By the blood of the Lamb, I command you to leave! You are defeated, by the power of the Cross, you are cast out!"

Jessica's body began to calm down, with her breath evening out and her trembling ceased. Her screams subsided into soft whimpers. The black mist, once so thick and menacing, began to dissolve, retreating into the shadows from which it had come. Pam and Tom held onto each other, tears streaming down their faces as they continued to pray. I noticed, I still had a death grip on Pam's arm and released her immediately, feeling guilty at the red marks left behind. I could see the relief in their eyes, and the hope that maybe, just maybe, this nightmare was finally coming to an end.

Just as everything settled down, the demon who was hiding in ambush showed he was not done yet. With a final, desperate act of defiance, it lashed out, throwing one last wave of darkness over the room. The lights flickered wildly, the walls trembled, and a deafening roar filled the air. Jessica screamed one last time, her voice filled with a pain that was almost too much to bear.

And then, just as suddenly as it had begun, it was over.

The Final Showdown

The oppressive darkness lifted, replaced by a calm that seemed almost surreal after the chaos we had just endured. The lights steadied, and the room fell into an eerie silence. Jessica lay on the floor, her body still, her breathing shallow but steady. Pam and Tom hovered close, their faces etched with concern and fear. As I touched Jessica's forehead, I felt a warmth, a peace that seemed to radiate from her very being. The demon's hold on her had been broken.

With a final prayer of thanks, I stood up, helping Pam and Tom to their feet. We looked around the room, taking in the mess left in the wake of the battle. But despite the broken furniture, the shattered glass, and the lingering chill in the air, there was a sense of peace that filled the house, a calm that had not been there before.

Tom picked up Jessica, holding her close as she began to stir. Her eyes fluttered open, and she looked up at her father with a confused expression. "Daddy?" she whispered, her voice small and weak.

Tom choked back a sob, hugging her tightly. "I'm here, sweetheart. I'm here."

Final Victory and Aftermath

The battle was fierce, and the demon fought with everything it had, but in the end, the power of God proved stronger. After what felt like hours of intense spiritual warfare, the demon's hold on Jessica finally broke. With a final, blood-curdling scream, the darkness lifted, and Jessica collapsed into her father's arms, sobbing but free.

The house fell silent, the oppressive atmosphere gone, replaced by a peaceful calm. The temperature returned to normal, and the foul smell vanished. Tom, Pam, and Jessica were shaken, exhausted, but alive and more importantly, they were free.

In the days that followed, the Hargroves began to heal. The strange occurrences stopped, and the house became a place of peace once more. Jessica slowly returned to the happy, playful child she had been before, though she had no memory of the events that had transpired that day.

Tom and Pam swore they would never play with the Ouija board and anything else that might be connected to the occult. They continued attending church regularly, strengthening their faith and their relationship with God. They knew now that what they had thought was a harmless game had nearly destroyed their family, and they were determined never to let such darkness into their lives again.

As for me, I was grateful to have been able to help them find freedom from the darkness that had tried to consume them. It was a reminder that the spiritual world is very real and that we must be careful not to open doors that we do not fully understand. The Hargroves learned that lesson the hard way, but in the end, they found their way back to the light.

Reflecting on the Battle

The experience with the Hargrove family was a stark reminder of the thin veil that separates our world from the spiritual realm. It taught me that we must always be vigilant, for the enemy is cunning and will use any opportunity to sow discord and destruction. The Ouija board, a seemingly harmless game, became the gateway for a malevolent spirit to enter their lives, wreaking havoc and bringing them to the brink of despair.

As a deliverance minister, I am constantly reminded of the importance of faith and prayer. As it is through these that we find our strength and our protection against the forces of darkness. The battle is never easy, but with God on our side, we know that victory is assured.

For the Hargroves, this ordeal was a wake-up call. They realized that they had been living without a true understanding of the spiritual dangers around them. Now, they are stronger in their faith and more aware of the reality of spiritual warfare. Their story is a testament to the power of God's love and the protection that comes from living a life grounded in faith.

Conclusion: A Warning to All

The story of the Hargroves serves as a warning to all who might consider dabbling in the occult or treating spiritual matters lightly. The spiritual world is not a game, and the forces at play are far more real and dangerous than most people realize. What starts as innocent curiosity or entertainment can quickly spiral into something far more sinister, with consequences that can last a lifetime in the case of generational curses, more than a lifetime.

If there is one thing I hope people take away from this story, it is that we must always be careful about the doors we open. We must stay vigilant, rooted in our faith, and always seek God's guidance and protection. For while the battle against darkness is real, so too is the victory that we have through Christ.

The Hargroves found their way back to the light, and their story serves as a beacon of hope for others who might find themselves in similar situations. It is a reminder that no matter how dark things may seem, there is always a way out, a path to freedom and healing through the love and power of God.

Chapter 6

The Seduction of Darkness

Note: This chapter contains content related to sexual violence that may be distressing for survivors.

Introduction to the Parker Family

Let me share with you the story of Michael and Jenny Parker, a couple who had been married for nearly fifteen years. They had two kids, a nice home, and from the outside, they appeared to have the perfect life. But beneath the surface, their marriage was crumbling as Michael, a successful businessman, had fallen into temptation. His long hours at work had led to lonely nights, and eventually, he began seeking solace in the arms of other women.

These affairs were something Michael kept hidden, locked away in the darkest corners of his heart, thinking that what Jenny didn't know wouldn't hurt her. But sin has a way of inviting darkness into our lives, and in Michael's case, that darkness took the form of a succubus—a demonic entity that feeds on lust and infidelity. What Michael didn't realize was that his actions had opened a door, inviting this entity not just into his life, but into his home, and it wasn't long before the succubus turned its attention to Jenny.

During my ministry, I have worked on numerous cases involving incubi and succubi, or sex demons. These often attach themselves through activities such as looking at porn, practicing forbidden sex acts, or committing adultery. These demons are very possessive of their property and are just as likely to attack someone they might see as a rival, such as a girlfriend or a wife. This was the case with Michael and Jenny, as Jenny became the focus of Michael's succubus.

First Signs of Demonic Activity

Jenny was the first to notice that something was wrong. It began with a feeling of unease, and a sense that she was being watched even when she was alone. At night, she would hear whispers, which were soft at first, like the rustle of fabric, but soon they grew louder, and more insistent. The air in the house felt thick, oppressive, as if something unseen was always lurking just out of sight.

Jenny started having strange dreams which were dark, twisted nightmares where she would be pursued by a shadowy figure that filled her with terror. She would wake up drenched in sweat, heart pounding, and though she would try to shake it off, the fear lingered. She began to notice bruises on her body, and marks that she couldn't explain. At first, she thought she might have bumped into something in the night, but as the bruises grew more frequent and more painful, she started to realize that something far more sinister was at play. Like most modern people who have no tuck with the supernatural, she was suddenly scared that she had cancer. She had a cousin who had died of leukemia and showed the same symptoms.

She made an appointment immediately with her personal doctor who was also alarmed by the bruising and marks but could find no biological cause. Tests that were sent out showed no sign of any physical malignancy. Though reassured that the wounds were not cancerous in nature, Jenny was left with a sense of impending danger and was about to realize how right she was.

The worst of it came one night when Jenny was alone in bed. Michael was away on a business trip, or so he said, and Jenny had just settled down for the night. She had drunk some of her favorite lavender and chamomile tea to help her relax. Bath bombs and late-night television were a great somnambulistic routine. She was drifting off to sleep when she felt a sudden pressure on her chest, as if someone was sitting on her. Scared, she tried to reach over to turn on the lamp to remove the darkness from the room. She tried to move, but her body wouldn't respond in the slightest. She was paralyzed, frozen with her eyes wide open, but seeing nothing. Her heart racing as a cold, slimy presence slithered over her skin.

Then, it happened. Jenny felt something—someone—holding her down, forcing itself upon and then into her. It was a violent, brutal assault by an unseen force. She tried to scream, to move, to fight back, but no sound came out and she was powerless to stop it. She could only lie there, helpless, as this malevolent entity had its way with her and violated her in the most horrific way. She was stripped of her basic humanity and treated like a thing. Tears poured down her cheek as the attack continued for what felt like hours. Then as suddenly as it started, it stopped. Jenny could move and she curled in a fetal ball; held tightly to her desecrated body, and cried, knowing she would never be same. When the shock of the attack started to wane, Jenny lay trembling, tears streaming down her face, feeling utterly violated and alone.

Escalation of Attacks

The attacks didn't stop there. Each night, Jenny would feel the presence in her room, watching her, waiting. The entity would torment her with whispers, promising to return, threatening to harm her if she ever told anyone. It was no longer just when she was in bed alone as it would press her against the wall in the shower and take her there, leaving her laying on the drain floor spent and crying. While sitting on the sofa an invisible hand would grasp her breast in a painful grip causing her gasp in intense pain and fear or when standing at the kitchen counter making a sandwich, her buttocks would be smashed as something would push her against the counter while forcibly rubbing her intimate parts. Jenny's health began to deteriorate. She couldn't sleep, couldn't eat, and the stress was taking a toll on her mind and body. She felt as though she was losing her grip on reality as her once peaceful home now a place of fear and torment. She skipped showering to avoid the attacks and tried wearing clothing to bed only to find herself stripped violently by the unseen entity causing her more damage as her clothing was ripped forcibly from her body.

Michael returned home from his "business trip" to find his wife a shell of her former self. She was pale, gaunt, and terrified of being left alone. Jenny tried to tell him what was happening, but the words stuck in her throat. How could she explain the horror she had experienced? How could she tell him about the unseen force that had violated her without sounding insane? It was a known fact that Jenny's grandmother had been institutionalized numerous times in her life because of schizophrenia as two of her sisters. Saying anything would only probably end up with Jenny in the same situation.

But the succubus wasn't content with just attacking Jenny. It began to visit Michael as well, though in a different way. At night, he would have vivid, erotic dreams of strange women, seductive and alluring. The dreams were so real that he would wake up feeling as though he had physically been with them and more than once having a "wet" dream. Considering the lack of attention, he was getting from his wife who seemed to flinch away at his touch, he didn't really mind. But these dreams soon turned dark. The women in his dreams became demonic, their eyes glowing red, their hands like claws that dug into his flesh.

Staring into the darkness

Slowly, Michael began to realize that something was terribly wrong. The once pleasurable dreams turned into nightmares. The succubus started tormenting him, mocking him for his infidelity, and threatening to destroy everything he loved. Though he was dreaming, it felt very real and there was no way this was just a subconscious movie reel. He would wake up in a cold sweat, the echoes of the demon's laughter ringing in his ears.

Seeking Help and the Confession

One night, after a particularly brutal attack on Jenny which by which the demon pinned her down on her stomach, assaulting her from behind while her husband lay beside her seemingly dead asleep and without knowledge of the sheer terror and pain she was being subjected to, she made the decision to tell Michael everything. When the presence was finished and again left as quickly as it attacked, Jenny grabbed Michael and shook him violently, attempting to wake him. Little did she know that Michael was caught in trapped terror of his own with the nightmares no longer mocking him verbally but assaulting him sexually in the dream. Like the sudden popping of a balloon, Michael sprang awake, sweating and panting in fear. He lookup up into the defeated eyes of his wife as she broke down and told him everything. She told him about the assaults, the terror she felt every night, and the presence that was destroying their lives. Michael listened, horrified, as the realization dawned on him that his actions had brought this evil into their home.

Overcome with guilt and shame, Michael confessed to Jenny about the affairs. He not only admitted that he had been unfaithful, but that he had been watching porn every night while getting off on what he saw. He figured that it was his lust that had somehow opened the door to this demonic entity but was still skeptical. Even with everything that had happened, Michael was a realist and dealt with the real world. Monsters did not exist in the real world and invisible creatures only violated people in books and movies. Yet, one look at the shell of a person that was left of his wife and seeing the pain in her eyes, he knew this was no movie. Something evil had come into their life, and he was the cause. Jenny was devastated by what he told her, but there was no time for anger or blame. They needed help, and they needed it fast.

Neither of them was particularly religious so they did not know exactly where to start. Jenny called the local catholic church because that seemed the thing to do in the movies. The priest seemed sympathetic but told them there was really nothing he could do. Jenny burst into tears at the end of her mental rope, as she had no idea what to do next. Seeing her anguish, the good father was shaken to his core.

"Let me make some phone calls to some of my peers in the area", he stated reaching for the phone. When after multiple calls, a local pastor that had worked with me got me through to Jenny. When they talked to me sitting in the basement of a local church, I could hear the desperation in their voices. They were at their breaking point, terrified that the next attack might be the last.

When I arrived at their home, I could feel familiar pain beneath my left shoulder blade. Many years prior, I had dealt with my own demonic attachment, and this is where it had set up shop. I had one time been addicted to porn through the influence of a sex demon and only freed through deliverance. Anytime I was confronted with porn or in an investigation dealing with a sex demon, I would get an uncomfortable or painful place near my left shoulder blade where the demon exited. I could tell that the darkness had taken root there. It was a suffocating presence, one that fed on the fear, guilt, and sinful pleasure that filled the house. Michael and Jenny looked like they hadn't slept in days with their faces pale and drawn. The fear in their eyes was unmistakable. Sex demons though not as powerful as witchcraft, satanic worship, or murder demons, were some of the most psychologically and physically brutal.

I began with prayer, asking God for protection and for the strength to confront the evil that had invaded their lives. I was well aware of the darkness I was walking into, and I was not eager to get back there.

The Battle with the Succubus

As I prayed, the succubus made its presence known. The room filled with a thick, oppressive darkness, and I could feel the demon's hatred directed at me. It lashed out, trying to disrupt the prayer, causing as impure thoughts and past porn views flashed through my mind. Many people don't realize it, but demons are incredibly intelligent and social creatures of their own. They talk and share past experiences. This creature was able to immediately attack me on my weak point and pulled up memories of times past. This is why many people that are knowledgeable of the field stay away. A demon will openly discuss your past and if you have not repented of these things and come to realize that it is no longer who you are, but that you are a new creature in Christ Jesus, you start down a rabbit hole that is hard to climb out of. But this was not my first rodeo, so I continued, refusing to back down.

Days before we met at the home, we had met at a local church to do primary investigations and discuss methods for dealing with the demonic. In my ministry, I always try to meet victims at a church which only presents a problem at times if the demon is in full possession. I have never had any issued there because the way I see it, I am a child of God and there is no way anyone is messing with one of God's kids in his house. Prior to meeting with me, the demon had gone on full attack mode to the point that they almost cancelled the meeting. Jenny had been brutally victimized with Michael observing for the first time yet being helpless to stop it. It was showing its full power over the couple and flaunting its strength. It warned them that if they met with me, it would get many times worse. With Michael and Jenny already at their breaking point, this thought almost shoved them over the end. Once done, it has assured them that things would be so much better if they no longer fought and just gave over. It was doing its utmost to move to full possession before the intervention.

Jenny had almost given in, as she just couldn't conceive of the situation getting worse. It was Michael, knowing that he was the one responsible for all the pain and torture his wife was enduring, who was willing to do anything to get rid of it. After much discussion about grace and God's love for them, I managed to guide them through the sinner's prayer. Each of them gave their lives to Christ that day in the church's basement, but as many have come to realize, that is not a supernatural forcefield against demons.

As a believing, Spirit-filled pastor, I had lived with a demonic attachment for years because of my own ignorance of the supernatural world and the rules involved. It makes me angry when I think about the disservice our church does to the bride of Christ in the lack of preparation it provides for spiritual warfare.

As Jenny and Michael knelt beside me, praying desperately as the demon began to attack. Jenny suddenly screamed as she felt invisible fingers touching her. Michael cried out, his voice breaking as he begged for forgiveness, pleading with God to save them from this nightmare. I knew something was off as there had been repentance and both had declared their lives for Christ. The demon should have been weaker but seemed not only powerful but pissed off. I prayed for divine insight on what was holding deliverance back, but nothing was touching my spirit. The only blessing was that it was more outward show than physical. It would touch and caress Jenny, yet nothing violent. Michael was being completely ignored. I knew that this was an important detail but could not figure out what was the problem. As the situation was not yet under control, I could not bless the house. Without full deliverance, forcing the demon out would only be a temporary fix and only lead to a much worse result in the end. With suggestions for playing praise music and prayers, I left.

The succubus turned its attention to me. That night, as I lay in bed after the deliverance session, I was visited by the demon in my dreams. It appeared as a beautiful woman, seductive and alluring, trying to tempt me, to draw me into its web. But I knew what it was, and I wasn't about to let it win. In the dream, the succubus approached me, its eyes glowing with an unnatural light. It reached out, its touch cold as ice, trying to pull me into darkness. I knew it was a dream, but I had been ambushed by the hag. I wanted to move, but I couldn't. I wanted to scream, but only a weak hum came from me. I could now feel my wife shaking me, asking me to wake up, but I was not able to respond. As the hag wrapped its arms around me, I screamed, "I rebuke you in Jesus's name!"

Staring into the darkness

The succubus shrieked, recoiling as if struck by an unseen force. I repeated the words, louder this time, feeling the power of Christ surge through me. "I rebuke you in Jesus's name! The demon let out a final, furious scream before vanishing, the dream dissolving into nothingness. I woke up with a start but victorious. The succubus had been driven back, but I knew it would return. My wife's beautiful face was concerned as she claimed, "I knew you were in trouble. I could hear you trying to scream and almost nothing came out. You wouldn't wake up. It was the hag again, wasn't it?".

I pulled her too me and told her it was okay and yes it was the hag again. I didn't know if I was every going to be free of her, but at least now, through the blood of Christ, I knew how to deal with her.

Over the next few nights, the succubus tried again and again to attack me in my dreams, each time taking on different forms, each time more desperate to break my resolve. But every time, I drove it off by rebuking it in the name of Jesus Christ. The battle was exhausting, but I knew I couldn't stop—not until the demon was gone for good. I knew this was not about me, but about trying to get me to desert the Parkers. If they got me distracted or weak then they could easily bring the Parkers back into the fold with violence and threats. They were not mature enough in their walk to withstand further attacks.

Final Victory and Aftermath

The final confrontation came during a powerful deliverance session at the Parkers' home. With Michael and Jenny by my side, we prayed with everything we had, calling on the power of Christ to banish the succubus from their lives forever. I continued to pray about what was holding full deliverance back but so far there was nothing. The demon fought back with all its might, touching, threatening, and causing an oppressive, dark presence to surround us. With this type of demon, it is not the heavy weight of oppression, but a type of enticement. It is very hard to describe in that it is trying to get you to let it help you. If you just allow it to help you, everything will be better. It is the age-old battle of the temptress discussed by Solomon in proverbs. There is a sweetness promised that will only end in pain and death. But we pressed on, our voices rising in prayer, refusing to give in to the fear. The succubus shrieked, its form becoming visible as a dark, twisted shadow writhing in the center of the room.

Michaeal asked "What does it want? What can we do to make it leave? We prayed the prayers and repented. I've confessed what I did, so why won't it leave us alone".

Jenny looked at him with scorn. "Did you think it was going to be that easy? Say some words and poof, everything is okay? Do you know what it's like being held down and having something rape you over and over? Take from you what's most private? I saw you dammit. I saw you when that thing raped me and made you watch. I saw you get aroused as it took everything from me. You son of a bitch, how could you? Wasn't it enough to cheat on me with another woman. To come home and hold me just after leaving her bed, but then get aroused at me getting raped by that thing." She was crying, tears streaming down her face as she tore lose the Band-Aids she had placed over her feelings. Emotions and words she had held back because there were worse things in front of her.

"I loved you, and you let that thing violate me? came out in a whisper. "I hate you, for what you did, and I hate myself because I love you." Michael was frozen in shock by the emotional outburst. I now had the answer I was looking for and it was time to move.

Jenny's looked at the floor as her tears fell freely. The succubus laughed and the darkness seemed to throb. You learn quickly in this field that marriage is the one pure thing to come out of the Garden of Eden. Man and woman became one in front of God the creator. That marriage came out of Eden with Adam and Eve. It is the pure and holy thing that the powers of evil have tried to destroy forever. This is why it is abomination to lie with members of the same sex. This is why divorce is so prevalent. The succubus does not infiltrate them to harass the people though that is a bonus. The succubus destroys the marriage. That is the goal.

I looked at Jenny and raised her chin. She looked so lost that my heart ached for her. This sweet child of God who had been brought into this millennia long war through no fault of her own but had suffered so much. This is the dichotomy of the deliverance field in that you can have so much love for someone like Jenny and be so angry at the demons who would hurt her so badly at the same time.

"You blame Michael for all of this, don't you", I asked taking her hands in mine.

"It's his fault. He did this. He was with other women when he said he loved me. How could he do that to me", she questioned

"There is no question that he sinned against God and the vows he made to you both, but we all have sinned and fallen short of the Glory of God. But he forgives us for our sins, wipes our tears, and picks us up when we fall. I'm going to need you to search the depths of your heart and forgive Michael for what he's done. I am not saying you need to condone it, or say it was okay, but I need you to forgive him. It's the only way you are going to be free and reclaim your life. Adulty was only the door that let the demon in, but it is staying based on this stronghold of hate and unforgiveness. Michael actions brought it here but it is staying by feeding on your hate."

"I don't know if I can. It hurt me so bad. I want him to hurt as badly as it hurt me. How come what he did was the sin that brought it here, but I had to suffer the worst? Why didn't it just attack him and leave me alone?", she cried.

I smiled as she suddenly looked like a young girl caught with her hand in the cookie jar. "Because regardless of what he did, hurting you and having him know it was because of him was worse than any physical pain it could have caused him. The physical pain will dim in time, but the psychological damage done by guilt and the wedge driven between the two of you may never heal. Even if you cannot do it for him, do it for you. Even if the demon left, you will never heal if you don't forgive him and release the hate. It will eat what is left of you until there is nothing left."

She paused so long that I was beginning to doubt that I had gotten through to her. Then she looked at Michael and stated, "I forgive you for what you've done to me and our marriage. I am not promising what things will look like from here on, as I don't know how I can look at you with the love I had before, but I forgive you."

In my spirit, I knew the stronghold was broken. "In the name of Jesus Christ, I command you to leave this house and never return!" I shouted, releasing Jenny and spreading my hands toward the presence, the words of scripture pouring from my lips.

The succubus let out a final, blood-curdling scream as it was forced out, the darkness lifting from the room, the oppressive atmosphere dissolving into nothingness. The house was still, the air warm and peaceful once more. Michael and Jenny collapsed toward each other. When Michael tried to wrap his arms around her, Jenny flinched but finally acquiesced, sobbing with relief.

In the weeks that followed, the Parkers began to heal, both from the spiritual attack and from the wounds left by Michael's infidelity. They sought counseling—both spiritual and marital—and worked together to rebuild the trust that had been shattered. They began to be discipled at a great church that had couples' groups. The darkness that had invaded their home was gone, replaced by the light of God's love and forgiveness.

Michael and Jenny dedicated their lives to God, with Michael vowing to remain faithful to his wife and to never again allow temptation to lead him astray. Jenny, though still hurt, found the strength to forgive him, and together they began the long journey toward healing.

As for me, it was a while before the succubus returned to my dreams. Sadly, this was a thorn in the side that I had created. It had been defeated, driven away by the power of Christ. The battle had been fierce, but in the end, light triumphed over darkness, and the Parkers' marriage was saved.

This case was a stark reminder of the dangers that lurk in the shadows, waiting for an opportunity to destroy. But it also reinforced the truth that no matter how dark the night, the light of Christ is always stronger, always victorious.

And so, the Parkers' home, once a place of fear and torment, became a sanctuary of peace and love, a testament to the power of faith and the strength of a marriage restored.

Chapter 7

The Wages of Sin

Introduction to the Carters

The story of Peter and Rachel Carter is one that still haunts me. It's a stark reminder of the consequences that can follow decisions made in moments of fear and desperation. They were a young couple, married for just a few years, when Rachel found out she was pregnant. It wasn't planned, and they weren't ready or at least, that's what they told themselves. They both had careers they were focused on, they wanted to travel, and they just didn't feel prepared to become parents. So, after much discussion, they made a choice they would both come to regret deeply; they decided to terminate the pregnancy. It wasn't an easy decision, and it was one that they kept a secret from their family, but they convinced themselves it was for the best. They were doing what they thought was right for their future, but what they didn't realize was that this decision would open the door to something dark and insidious.

The First Signs of Trouble

In the months following the abortion, things began to change in their relationship. The once happy and loving couple started to drift apart. Rachel became distant, withdrawn, and prone to sudden bouts of sadness that she couldn't explain. Peter, on the other hand, threw himself into his work, trying to escape the growing tension at home. They never spoke about what they had done, hoping that by burying it, they could move on. But the guilt and shame lingered, festering in the shadows of their minds.

They began to argue and brood more than talk to each other. Small things started to occur which would then set off a major argument which would then lead to resentment and separation. Each day when he came home from work, Peter would place his keys in the drawer by the door along with his wallet and pen. Then he would collect them on his way out the door. One Saturday as he was preparing to go the store, he opened the drawer and his keys were missing. He sighed in frustration.

"Honey, what did you do with my keys?", he yelled toward the back of the house where Rachel was watching TV.

"What?" she answered, confused.

"What the Hell did you do with my keys? If you needed to use them fine, but please put them back where you found them".

"I haven't touched your damn keys", she returned with an angry tone starting in her voice.

"You're full of shit", he yelled. "I know damn well I didn't move them and you're the only other person here?".

Rachel had now come into the room. "I told you I haven't touched your keys. You probably picked them up earlier and forgot where you put them. Just take mine if you're in such a hurry; they're in my purse".

"I don't want your keys; I want mine and I haven't picked them up since I got home yesterday evening. I know I put them right here like I always do." Peter let more anger come into his voice. "Are you fucking with me for some reason? Because if you are, I'm not laughing."

Rachel had had enough. "Screw you", she exclaimed as she headed by to the TV with tears in her eyes.

Peter seethed, but inside he knew he should not have reacted so harshly to Rachel. But dammit, she had to have moved his keys. Why couldn't she just admit she had moved them and forgot where she put them. He started walking around the house, looking for his keys. Her purse was hanging on the back of the kitchen chair, so he looked inside. Sitting right beside her keys were his.

"Fuckin knew it", he growled as he grabbed his keys and left, slamming the door after him.

Little things like keys missing, towels being left on the floor, or slippers being pushed deep under the bed which would have been a grunt and shake of the head most of their marriage now became screaming matches.

Staring into the darkness

Rachel also started waking up in the middle of the night with recurring nightmares. She would dream of a small, faceless child, crying out for her; reaching out with tiny hands that she couldn't bear to look at. Or she would find herself in a nursery and hear a baby crying. When she would reach the crib, there would be a dead child laying there, staring at her with empty eye sockets. She would wake up drenched in sweat, her heart racing, and no matter how hard she tried; she couldn't shake the feeling of overwhelming loss.

Peter's dreams were different, but equally disturbing. He dreamed of dark figures standing at the foot of his bed, whispering accusations. They told him that he had failed as a husband and as a father. He would wake up to the sound of those whispers still echoing in his ears, and the oppressive feeling that something was watching him would linger long after he opened his eyes. Occasionally he would see what he thought was flashes of darkness flit around to the room and into closets or under the dresser. Checking his phone by the bed, the nightmares were on a constant pace waking him between two and three each morning. Once awake, there was no returning to sleep. A solid night's sleep had become a rare commodity for either of them.

Their home and marriage, once refuges of warmth and love, became a prison of guilt and fear. They would fight over the smallest things, arguments that would escalate quickly and leave both feeling more isolated than ever. And then the physical attacks began.

Rachel would wake up with bruises on her arms and legs, and mysterious scratches on random parts of her body. At first, she tried to explain them away as maybe she had bumped into something at work in the garden center. She was always loading mulch or moving plants around. It was probably made from roses. But deep down, she knew something was terribly wrong.

The Spiral into Despair

As the attacks grew more intense and her marriage started to unravel, Rachel turned to alcohol to numb the pain and silence the nightmares. It started with a glass of wine in the evening to help her sleep, but soon it escalated to drinking before heading to work and starting as soon as she got home. The alcohol had become her only escape from the relentless torment. Peter noticed Rachel was drinking way more than before, of course, but he was struggling with his own demons. If he mentioned anything, it became World War III and he just didn't have the energy to fight. He didn't know how to help her, so he ignored it, hoping it was just a phase and that she would snap out of it.

But Rachel didn't snap out of it. She spiraled deeper into her addiction with her once vibrant personality fading into a shadow of who she used to be. Her work suffered and she had been written up twice for being late. Her boss had noticed a definite change in her behavior and attitude and tried to suggest help with the company's

Staring into the darkness

EAP, but The alcohol dulled the fear for a while, but it also made the attacks more frequent, more violent. She would wake up in the middle of the night to the feeling of cold hands gripping her, pulling her down into darkness. She would scream, but the sound would die in her throat, strangled by an unseen force.

Her health began to deteriorate rapidly. She lost weight, her skin became pale and sallow, and the light in her eyes dimmed. Desperate to break free, Rachel checked herself into a rehab facility, hoping that by getting sober, she could reclaim her life. But the attacks followed her there.

The staff at the rehab center chalked up her episodes to alcohol withdrawal. They told her that the hallucinations and nightmares were just her body's way of coping with the sudden absence of alcohol. But Rachel knew better. The attacks were real, and they were getting worse. She would wake up in the middle of the night to find her room freezing cold with the walls closing in on her. The dark presence she had felt at home now looming over her, in the cold soulless rehab room, threatening to consume her entirely.

She stayed in rehab for as long as she could, but she only seemed to get worse as the constant attacks wore her down. The staff couldn't help her, and the therapy sessions seemed useless against the relentless onslaught of terror. She was hearing voices telling her to kill herself and that the world would be better off without her. There was no way she could admit that to the staff or in group as they would lock her down for suicide ideations. Eventually, Rachel was released, and she returned home, but she wasn't the same. The moment she walked through the door, the oppressive atmosphere of the house seemed to close in on her, and it wasn't long before she turned back to alcohol for comfort. At least if she passed out, she felt she was free from the torment for a little while.

But in time, the alcohol wasn't enough. The darkness in the house was stronger now, feeding off her fear and guilt, and it pushed her to the brink of despair. One night, Peter and she had just had another fight and as he left, he said "I don't know why I even come back here,". As he slammed the door and walked away, unable to bear the torment any longer, Rachel made a decision that would nearly cost her life. She mixed a handful of barbiturates with a bottle of vodka, hoping to end the pain once and for all.

She had lost her child, her husband, and her job. She felt she had nothing left in life. Peter came back home and found her just in time. He had been out walking the streets, trying to understand what had happened to their perfect life. Where had it all gone wrong? He had been walking for almost an hour when it started to rain a cold, body chilling rain. He figured if he was going to be completely miserable, he may as well go home. At least he would be miserable while being warm and dry. Peter returned home to find Rachel unconscious on the bathroom floor, the empty pill bottle and liquor bottle lying next to her. Panicked, he called 911, and she was rushed to the hospital.

Rachel's stomach was pumped while Peter cried in the waiting room. He thought about the last words he had spoken to the love of his life and was terrified that it would be the last words she would ever here. The doctors managed to save her life, but just barely. Later, the doctor said he could visit, and he stood outside the room for almost five minutes trying to muster up the courage to enter. As he saw her lying in the hospital bed, weak and broken, Peter realized that he was on the verge of losing everything.

Peter's Descent into Darkness

While Rachel was in rehab, Peter's own struggles with the demonic attacks intensified. The dark figures in his dreams became more aggressive, more threatening. They whispered lies into his ears, telling him that he was worthless. They told him that he had destroyed his wife's life, that he should just give up. The guilt and shame that had been eating away at him for months finally broke him, and he fell into a deep depression.

Unlike Rachel who had only started drinking after the attacks started, Peter had always enjoyed a good whiskey after work at the neighborhood bar while watch sports with his friends. As things had intensified, he found more and more excuses to visit the bar and found himself drinking more and more. At first, it was just to take the edge off, to help him get through the day. But as the depression grew darker, drinking became more frequent, more desperate. With Rachel gone, it was more convenient to stay at home. He would sit in the darkened living room, a bottle in his hand, drowning in his own misery while the shadows crept closer, whispering their poison into his ear.

When Rachel was released from the hospital, she found her husband a broken man. He was distant, cold, and consumed by the same darkness that had nearly destroyed her. The house was suffocating, filled with a sense of dread that neither of them could escape. They were both trapped in a cycle of guilt, fear, and despair, with no way out.

That's when they reached out to their pastor, a man named Jack who had known them for years. Like most Sunday Christians, calling out to the Lord was something done as a last resort instead of a first response. As he listened to all they said, Jack was deeply concerned. When he went to visit and saw the state they were in, he knew they needed help badly, and he knew that this was beyond anything he could handle on his own. That's when he called me.

Jack and I had been friends for a long time, and he knew about my work in deliverance ministry after I helped a pastor friend of his. When he called me, he didn't sugarcoat the situation. "Russ," he said, "this is bad. Real bad. I've never seen anything like it and if they don't get help of some kind, I don't think they will survive."

Staring into the darkness

The First Deliverance Session

As with most clients, I had them come to the church and we discussed their situation. I was not sure exactly what I was dealing with as they both were dealing with feelings of guilt and alcohol dependency which could very easily be confused for demonic activity. I was not getting anything on discernment and would have probably simply suggested continued mental health treatment if not for the admission about the abortion. For those who are not aware, there is almost nothing more abominable in the spiritual realm than the commission of abortion. For someone who is sensitive to spiritual evil, praying outside a clinic that does this is the worst. It can only be described as a demonic amusement park where the worst of Hell's beings reside. The feed off the foul acts and soulless depravity involved in killing of the most innocent. For this reason, I was surprised when I first visited their home. Peter and Rachel looked like they were barely holding on, their faces pale and gaunt, their eyes hollow, but I did not feel the normal oppressiveness and darkness. Yet years of experience had me spiritually looking over my shoulder as if I was taking a stroll across the open plains, waiting for a predator to jump out in ambush.

We sat down together, and again, they told me everything. The abortion, the guilt, the nightmares, the attacks, the drinking, and the suicide attempt. As they spoke, I could see the pain etched into their faces, the regret and shame that had consumed them. But I could also see something else; my discernment was just starting to warn me of something darker that was feeding off their suffering. This was different from the frontal attack I was met with most often during sessions. There was not the alpha predator attack that came with a blitz, hoping to overwhelm and cause me to leave. This had a patient aspect to it as if it thought if it waited long enough, I would leave on my own and it could continue to savor its banquet of fear and self-hatred.

If you watch too many movies or TV programs, it's almost that Hollywood wants you to think these creatures who have been here for thousands of years are stupid, feral beasts, just lashing out and must be beaten back into their spiritual cages. This thought process could not be farther from the truth. Demons for the most part are highly intelligent and very crafty. I knew that we were dealing with more than just the emotional aftermath of their decision. The demonic forces that had been unleashed by their actions were relentless, and they weren't going to leave without a fight. We needed to take this seriously, and we needed to start with a full-on deliverance session which often starts with some form of provocation. Obviously, my presence was not enough so it was time to step it up a notch.

I put the praise music CD in the stereo and began the session by praying together, asking for God's protection and guidance. As I prayed, I could feel the atmosphere in the room shift. The air grew colder, and the oppressive weight seemed to intensify, as if the demons were gathering their strength for the battle ahead. I had already tested both for possession and that was not the case. Neither had problems entering the church where we had the interviews and there was no reaction to the blessed St. Benedict ring or crucifix. This was a case where children had never learned to grow up and had let Satan fool them into thinking they were prey in the spiritual and physical realm. I spent time discussing the benefits of being children of the Living God, but I could tell this was not reaching them. Like so many, they did not have faith in the Word and as such did not get the benefits promised within. Both had repented of their sins and prayed the sinner's prayer without difficulty.

The problem is that their spirit was starving because it was never fed. Like anything else, without sustenance things weaken and often die. The human spirit will not die, but it will get weak without regular feedings of power and nourishment from the Heavenly realm. This is why listening to praise music, preaching, having fellowship, reading the Word of God, and most importantly developing a relationship with the Father through prayer, praise, and spending time with the Holy Spirit. Then when the attacks come, they are not facing a helpless child, but a full-grown warrior armed with the full armor of God and the Sword of the Word. This same sword Jesus used against Satan every time he came against our Lord and Savior. Jesus did not physically attack Satan, but stated "It is written…." He used the Sword of the Word.

As I started to bless the rooms of the house and command the demons to leave in the name of Jesus Christ, the room finally erupted in chaos. The lights dimmed, objects flew off shelves, and the temperature dropped even further. Peter and Rachel clung to each other; fear etched into their faces as the darkness seemed to close in around them. I told them, to not fear as that was what the demons wanted, have faith the in their Holy Father.

The demons fought back with everything they had. The whispers grew louder, more insistent, telling Peter and Rachel that they were worthless, that they didn't deserve to be free, that they were beyond redemption. I rebuked their lies, continuing to command that they had no power here and were bound in Heaven and Earth from causing harm. The more the commotion grew, refused to give in to the fear that was gnawing at the edges of my own mind. Too often we think that as Christians, we are immune to demonic attacks, but that is not true. Evan our Lord was tempted by Satan three times that were recorded. We will be bombarded by sights and sounds to distract us from carrying out the great commission of casting out devils.

"In the name of Jesus Christ, I command you to leave this house and these people!" I shouted, my voice cutting through the chaos. The demons shrieked in rage, the sound reverberating through the room, but I didn't back down. I knew that the power of Christ was greater than anything they could throw at us. Just like a muscle used in the gym, faith grows stronger with use. This is why Satan will attack new Christians to get them to either turn from the Word or put it at the end of the line. The example of Peter and Rachel were a great excuse of that by only seeking God's help at the end instead of the beginning. The best way not to get sick is to remain healthy from the start.

There were hideous sounds and smells all around. Shadows leapt, dodged, and darted around the room and directly at us, only to reflect away at the last second. Finally, after what felt like hours of intense spiritual warfare, the darkness began to lift. The temperature in the room started to rise, the lights steadied, and the oppressive weight seemed to dissipate. Peter and Rachel collapsed into each other's arms, tears streaming down their faces as they felt the first glimmer of hope in what seemed like an eternity. I had commanded the demons to depart to the feet of Jesus, to be dealt with as His wisdom deemed necessary.

The first deliverance session had been successful. The demons had been driven back, out of their house, and out of their lives. For a while, the Carters seemed to be on the road to recovery spiritually and physically. They stopped drinking entirely, started attending church regularly, sought counseling, and worked on rebuilding their marriage. For a time, it seemed like they had turned a corner.

The Return of Darkness

But the battle was far from over, because as many people are mistaken about deliverance being an event like an exorcism, it is not. Deliverance is a lifestyle as much as sobriety or recovery. Once you have been under demonic oppression, it is always right there. You have beaten and angered creatures thousands of years old who have a hatred for mankind that our minds cannot fathom. You see, they fell and can never receive Grace for their mistake. Their future is an eternity in the lake of fire that was created for them. Humans on the other hand, can repent of their mistakes and be brought back into God's Grace with forgiveness.

A few months after the first deliverance session, Peter and Rachel had a massive argument. The stress of everything they had been through, combined with the lingering guilt and unresolved issues, led to a blowout fight that left both of them reeling. As he had before, Peter stormed out of the house and that night, Peter did something he hadn't done in months—he reached for a bottle. He told himself it was just one drink to calm his nerves, but that one drink quickly turned into several. Before he knew it, he was drunk, and the darkness that had been lurking in the background came rushing back in. When he returned home with a three-fourths empty bottle of whiskey, Rachel could smell the alcohol on his breath and tore into him. She screamed in anger at not only Peter's actions but the possible outcome for her still being in sobriety. How dare he bring alcohol back into their home.

Then the unthinkable happened and Peter pushed Rachel out of his way, causing her to trip over the ottoman and hit the floor hard. The physical damage was nothing to the emotional damage done in an instant. In all their years of marriage, Peter had never physically harmed her. He had always been a gentle soul. Yet even as she lay on the floor in shock and unable to move, he simply turned away and walked to his office where he shut the door. Rachel lay there and wept.

The demons, sensing that their opportunity had returned, attacked with vengeance. That night, whispers returned, louder and more menacing than before, telling Peter that he was a failure, that he didn't deserve forgiveness because he was so weak, that he should just give up and leave. The shadows in the house grew darker, more oppressive, and the attacks on Rachel resumed with a new intensity.

Rachel, who had been doing so well in her recovery, was devastated by Peter's relapse. She tried to stay strong, but the relentless attacks wore her down. The bruises and scratches returned, the nightmares became more frequent, and she felt as though she was being dragged back into the pit she had fought so hard to escape.

It wasn't long before she turned back to alcohol as well, desperate to numb the pain and silence the voices that whispered to her in the dark. The cycle of addiction and despair that had nearly destroyed them before was starting all over again, and this time, it seemed even more hopeless.

The Second Deliverance Session

When I received the call from Jack, I could tell from his voice that things had taken a turn for the worse. "Russ," he said, "it's happening again. They need you."

I returned to the Carters' home, and the moment I walked through the door, I knew that the darkness had regained its hold. The air was thick with tension, and Peter and Rachel looked even worse than before. Only this time, there was something different. The fear in their eyes was back, and I could see that the demons had been working overtime to break them but there was a separation to them that was not there before.

We gathered in the living room, and I could feel the oppressive presence in the room, stronger than ever. This time, the demons weren't just feeding off their guilt—they were feeding off the despair and hopelessness that had taken root in their hearts.

We began praying, but this time the demons were even more resistant. The room shook, the temperature dropped, and the whispers grew louder, more insistent. The demons taunted Peter and Rachel, telling them that they were beyond saving, that they were failures in God's kingdom, and should just embrace the darkness.

But we pressed on, refusing to give in to the fear. I could see the pain in Peter's eyes, as he confessed the regret for letting the demons back into his life, for physically assaulting his wife. I knew that he was on the edge of breaking. I prayed with everything I had, calling on the power of Christ to drive the demons out once and for all.

The battle was intense, and at times it felt like we were losing. But finally, after what felt like hours of struggle, the darkness began to lift once more. Peter and Rachel collapsed but unlike last time, it was not into each other's arms. Peter sat in a kitchen chair while Rachel simply hugged herself, tears streaming down their faces as they felt the first glimmer of hope return but the possible permanent loss of something they may never get back.

The second deliverance session had been successful, but I knew that they couldn't let their guard down. The demons had been driven back, but they weren't gone. They would never be truly gone and were waiting for another opportunity. Now that there was an added stressor in their lives and on their marriage, this fight would be even harder. I warned Peter and Rachel that they needed to be vigilant and work together to not let the darkness back into their lives.

The Final Confrontation

For a time, things seemed to improve. Peter and Rachel were both attending counseling, working on their marriage, and trying to stay strong in their faith. But the darkness was always lurking in the background, waiting for a moment of weakness. That moment came one night when Peter and Rachel had another argument. It wasn't as intense as the one that had led to Peter's relapse, but it was enough to crack the fragile peace they had built. When Peter started for the door, Rachel asked if he was going to find his liquid courage again so he could come back and beat her. Rachel regretted the words as soon as she said them as she saw the effect on Peter was as if she had hit him with a bat. He staggered, feeling the weight of the guilt of what he had done before as tears welled up. He walked slowly out the door down the street and in the land of self-hate, the pressure to stay sober weakened and reached for a bottle once again.

This time, he stopped himself after just one drink, but the damage was done. Only this time, it was not just the whiskey, but the torn marriage, self-loathing, feelings of not being good enough. The demons, sensing their opportunity, attacked with a ferocity that was unlike anything before.

Rachel was the first to be attacked. She woke up in the middle of the night to the feeling of her mentally being grabbed by cold hands pulling her down into darkness. She screamed, but the sound was strangled in her throat, as the demonic presence pressed down on her, trying to spiritually suffocate her. Peter rushed to her side, but he was immediately overwhelmed by the darkness. It was a blitz attack. Like predator's searching out prey, the demons could sense the hopelessness and despair between them. The demons attacked him, dragging him down into a pit of despair and hopelessness. He could feel the weight of his guilt crushing him, the whispers telling him that he was a failure, that he didn't deserve to be free.

Desperate and terrified, Peter and Rachel called me in the middle of the night, begging for help. When I arrived, the house was a battleground. The air was thick with the presence of evil, and the atmosphere was charged with a sense of impending doom. This was I was hoping the final confrontation, and I knew that if we didn't succeed this time, the demons would probably destroy them both.

We gathered in the living room, and I began praying with everything I had. The demons fought back with vengeance, as they were angry at being denied a prize, they felt was theirs. The whispers were deafening, telling Peter and Rachel that they were beyond redemption, that they should just give up and that God could not protect them. But I refused to give in as I knew that the power of Christ was greater than anything these demons could throw at us. I prayed with all my strength, commanding the demons to leave in the name of Jesus Christ.

The battle raged on for what felt like an eternity. The demons were relentless, refusing to give up their hold on Peter and Rachel. But finally, after hours of intense spiritual warfare, the darkness began to lift, and we were again alone.

The Aftermath

I got back with Jack and insisted that the people helping Peter and Rachel put more time and effort into discipleship. This was not a phone call once a week situation but two lives and souls on the edge. Jack could see my anger at the failure of the church to nurture two spiritual children who were in need. He swore he would make sure that Peter and Rachel would receive all the spiritual guidance he could give and would do it himself.

In the days that followed, Peter and Rachel began to rebuild their lives once more with regular counseling form Jack and a local Christian counselor he recommended. The house, once a place of fear and torment, became a sanctuary of peace and love. They both rededicated their lives to God, vowing never to let the darkness back in. They continued to attend counseling, working on their marriage and their faith. They knew that the road to recovery would be long, but they were committed to walking it together.

I stayed in touch with them, offering support and guidance as they navigated the challenges ahead. I reminded them that they had been given a second, third and fourth chance, and that they needed to stay vigilant, to never allow the darkness to creep back into their lives.

As I left their home for the final time, I felt a sense of peace knowing that they were finally free. The battle had been fierce, but in the end, the light of Christ had triumphed over the darkness. Peter and Rachel had been saved, not just from the demonic forces that had tormented them, but from the despair and hopelessness that had nearly destroyed them and their marriage.

Their story is a powerful reminder of the consequences of our actions, but also of the boundless mercy and grace of God. No matter how far we may stray, no matter how deep the darkness may seem, there is always a way back to the light. Peter and Rachel found that way, and their lives were forever changed because of it.

Chapter 8

Introduction to Steven's Story

Steven Matthews was a man who believed he had a strong moral compass and firm control over his life. As a correctional counselor at a maximum-security prison, he worked primarily with sex offenders. Considering it was a parole requirement to attend his program for any chance of early release, Steven had met offenders from all levels. It was a challenging job, exposing him daily to the darkest and most depraved sides of human behavior. In order to know the participants, Steven had to read their individual files which included details of the crimes committed. This included everything from voyeurism, to pedophilia, to rage rape that left victims maimed or dead. But Steven saw himself as a protector, someone who could help guide these men back to a semblance of normalcy, so maybe they would no longer prey on others if released, even if he didn't always believe they could be fully rehabilitated.

Steven had been married to his high school sweetheart, Laura, for over fifteen years. He had been a correctional officer when they met and first married and through hard work and education been promoted to correctional counselor. They had been blessed with two young children and lived in a quiet suburban neighborhood. On the surface, they seemed like the perfect family. But beneath that veneer of normalcy, Steven's work was starting to take a toll on him, in ways he hadn't anticipated.

The Beginning of the Descent

It all began gradually. After long days at the prison, listening to detailed confessions and fantasy writings of the inmates, Steven would come home feeling unsettled, with a heavy weight on his chest. The stories he heard at work were graphic and horrific, filled with descriptions of abuse and perversion that stayed with him long after he left the prison. One inmate who had been convicted of raping his eleven-year-old niece denied the charge because he stated at eleven, she was too old for him, and he liked girls or boys younger. At first, Steven tried to shake it off by spending time with his family, immersing himself in hobbies, and try to focus on the good things in life. But the darkness seemed to follow him everywhere.

One evening, after a particularly grueling session with an inmate who had broken into a house, raped a forty-two-year-old wife while forcing the husband to watch. He then heard a noise upstairs and, to the parents' horror, brought down their seventeen-year-old daughter. The mother then begged him to do whatever he wanted to her, but not hurt the daughter. He then raped the mother brutally again while making the daughter watch. Such things were not made for a normal human mind to be exposed to. Steven found himself unable to sleep. He tossed and turned, his mind racing with the images that had been painted for him that day. Desperate for some form of escape, he turned to the internet, looking for something—anything—that would distract him.

He stumbled upon a pornographic website. It wasn't something he had looked at since he was in college; in fact, he had always considered himself above such things. But in that moment, the twisted thing that he had picked up from work convinced him that he just wanted to drown out the thoughts in his head. He clicked on a video and, for a brief moment, felt a sense of relief as the images on the screen replaced the images in his mind.

The Succubus Takes Hold

At first, Steven only watched porn occasionally, telling himself it was just a way to unwind after work. But soon, it became a nightly ritual. Plus, he kept telling himself that he was an adult, and everything was perfectly legal. At the same time, he made sure his office door was locked so his wife could not see what he was doing. Like any addiction, the standard videos were enough for a while, but as time went on, he found himself needing more extreme content to achieve the same effect. Regular if any porn can be considered regular, videos that once satisfied him no longer did the trick, and he began to seek out more deviant forms of pornography.

It wasn't long before Steven's tastes became darker. He started watching videos of violent sex, gang bangs, and then videos depicting rape fantasies. Girls being tied up, or held down, beaten and individually or gang raped. He told himself it was just fantasy, that it didn't mean anything, but the thrill he felt from watching these videos was unlike anything he had experienced before. It was intoxicating, addictive, and he found himself unable to stop.

As Steven's addiction grew, the content he consumed became more extreme. He started seeking out videos involving brutal violence, bondage, and humiliation. His values became so warped he found himself looking at rape scenes of vintage cartoon characters. Anything to feed this new dark need. He even stumbled upon videos depicting acts of incest and child exploitation, though he never allowed himself to watch those. The worst part is that he avoided them, not because he knew it was wrong, but because he was afraid he would end up on a list and be arrested. The thrill of the forbidden was hard to resist and getting harder every day.

What Steven didn't realize was that his exposure to this dark content was opening a door to something far more sinister. Unbeknownst to him, a succubus had attached itself to him, from his proximity to the sexual deviants he worked with, feeding off his growing lust and perversion. This demonic entity had been lurking in the shadows, waiting for the moment when Steven's defenses were down. And now, it had found its way in.

Dark Fantasies and Real-Life Consequences

The succubus began to manipulate Steven's thoughts, pushing him further and further into the darkness. The fantasies that had once been confined to the screen began to spill over into his real life. His once happy life with Laura was now no longer satisfying or happy. He started to fantasize about his wife, Laura, in ways he never had before. Their sex life once was easy and natural, but his ability to perform was lessened. He could only become aroused now by imagining her being violently raped by strange men who had broken into her house while he was away. Her cries for help fell on deaf ears while she was brutalized. He even fantasized about being tied up and being forced to watch while it happened.

One night, as Steven and Laura were being intimate, he found himself overcome with a sudden urge while his mind moved through depravity. Without thinking, he wrapped his hands around her throat and began to slowly squeeze. Laura's eyes widened in shock, and she tried to push him away, but Steven was lost in his fantasy, imagining her as a helpless victim. It wasn't until he saw the fear in her eyes that he snapped back to reality, immediately releasing her and backing away, horrified by what he had done.

"I'm sorry," he stammered, his hands shaking. "I don't know what came over me."

Laura was shaken but tried to reassure him. Not realizing the dark forces influencing her once loving husband. "It's okay, Steven," she said, though her voice was tinged with fear. "Let's just go to sleep."

But sleep was the last thing Steven could do. He lay awake all night, his mind racing with thoughts of what he had done. He knew something was terribly wrong, but the thought of what had happened left him so aroused he had to get up and relieve himself reliving the actions in his memory. He knew by trying to harm Laura, that his fantasies were spiraling out of control. He tried to convince himself that it was just stress, that it was the nature of his job getting to him. But deep down, he knew it was more than that and that something was wrong.

The Breaking Point

As Steven's addiction worsened, his thoughts became darker and more depraved. He found himself fantasizing about his sister-in-law, Jenny, a petite woman with a kind smile and a gentle demeanor. The fantasies started innocently enough with thoughts of what it might be like to be with her. He would daydream of them being left alone together and things just happening. But as the succubus tightened its grip on Steven, those fantasies grew more violent, more terrifying.

Steven began to imagine breaking into Jenny's house while her husband was away at work. He pictured her sleeping in her bed, unaware of the danger lurking just outside her door. He fantasized about sneaking up behind her, covering her mouth with his hand, and forcing himself on her. The thought of her screaming, crying, begging him to stop, filled him with a twisted sense of excitement.

He even went so far as to start planning it out. He knew Jenny's schedule, knew when her husband would be away, and knew where she kept the spare key. He imagined every detail, every horrific act he would commit, and the thought of it consumed him.

But it wasn't just Jenny. Steven's fantasies began to bleed into his everyday life as he found himself thinking about the women he saw on the street, wondering what it would be like to force himself on them, to make them his. The succubus was in full control now, whispering in his ear, feeding his darkest desires.

Realizing the Problem

The breaking point came one night when Steven woke up in a cold sweat, his heart racing. He had dreamed of Jenny again, but this time it wasn't just a fantasy. In the dream, he had actually broken into her house, just as he had planned. He had attacked her, brutally raping her, and when it was over, he had strangled her to death.

Steven bolted upright in bed, gasping for air, his mind reeling from the horror of what he had just dreamed. He looked over at Laura, sleeping peacefully beside him, and felt a wave of guilt and shame wash over him. He was becoming just like or worse than the men he counseled. He knew he was losing control, that his fantasies were turning into something far more dangerous. The horror of what he was becoming began to tear through him. Where would the fantasies end or would they. When would his depravity sink so low that he would even consider hurting his two young daughters. This thought was like a bucket of cold water being thrown on his consciousness. This ended now.

Desperate for help, Steven confided in Laura the next morning. He told her everything—the porn addiction, the violent fantasies, the dream about Jenny. There was no depravity he left hidden. He broke down in tears, confessing how lost and afraid he felt, how he didn't know who he was anymore and that he would rather take his own life than do what these thoughts were driving him toward.

Laura was horrified and disgusted by what she heard. At first she was furious, but she could see the pain in Steven's eyes, the desperation for help. She knew they needed to do something, and fast. She reached out to their pastor, an old friend of mine named Pastor James, and told him everything.

Calling in Pastor Russ

When Pastor James called me, he didn't mince words. "Russ, we've got a serious problem here. Steven needs help and he needs it now."

I agreed to meet with Steven and Laura that same day at the church for the initial interview and tests. Both had been church goers most of their lives and had both given their lives to Jesus many years ago. Once again met with the situation of Christians forgetting their first home. Churches are not doing their job of teaching the Truth. Baby

Christians are staying babies for decades because the tenders of the House of God are not weaning them with spiritual warfare doctrine and moving them to solid food. Even during out meetings and discussions where I tell them the real Truth of who they are in the spiritual kingdom and how they have authority if they will only have faith in the Word and take it, they still allow fear to rule and do not achieve what is rightfully theirs.

When I arrived at their home, I knew that something was off. It was setting my discernment bells ringing like a cathedral on Sunday. Steven looked like a man on the edge, his eyes hollow, his face pale and gaunt. Laura was holding his hand, trying to offer support, but I could see the fear and uncertainty in her eyes. It's one thing to think about your husband having a porn addiction, but quite another to come to the reality that you are being attacked by demons and that those boogeymen you grew up hearing about in stories are real and actively trying to destroy you.

We sat down together, and Steven told me everything. As he spoke, I could see the pain etched into his face, the shame and regret that had consumed him. But I could also see something else—something darker that was feeding off his suffering. I knew that we were dealing with more than just an addiction. The demonic forces that had been unleashed by his actions were relentless, and they weren't going to leave without a fight. We needed to take this seriously, and we needed to start with a full-on deliverance session.

Staring into the darkness

The First Deliverance Session

We began by praying together, asking for God's protection and guidance. As I prayed, I could feel the atmosphere in the room shift. The response of this defeated foe is always to attack. Their only defense is to get the people convinced that they are lost and are not citizens of heaven. They were defeated over 2000 years ago, but as much as they lie to others, they lie to themselves the most. They seem to think they have a chance against the King of Kings and Lord of Lords. The air grew colder, and the oppressive weight seemed to intensify, as if the demons were gathering their strength for the battle ahead.

As I commanded the demons to leave in the name of Jesus Christ, the room erupted in chaos. The lights flickered, objects flew off shelves, and the temperature dropped even further. Steven, Laura, and I held each other's hands with Laura's turning into a crushing grip as fear etched into their faces and the darkness seemed to close in around them.

The succubus fought back with everything it had. The whispers grew louder, more insistent, telling Steven that he was worthless, that he didn't deserve to be free, that he was beyond redemption. I could tell by the look on his face that he was seeing images in his mind to distract from focusing on Jesus. I pressed on, refusing to give in to the fear that was gnawing at the edges of my own mind and the sexual imagery that was bombarding my own mind. "In the name of Jesus Christ, I command you to leave this man and this house!" I shouted, my voice cutting through the chaos. The succubus shrieked in rage, its presence becoming more tangible, as if it were trying to manifest itself physically in the room. The lights flickered violently, and a cold wind seemed to whip through the room, even though all the windows were closed.

The atmosphere was thick with tension, and I could feel the evil force pushing back against my prayers. Steven's face contorted in pain as the succubus tightened its grip on him. He let out a low, guttural scream, clutching his head as if something was trying to tear him apart from the inside.

"Steven, stay with me!" I urged, reaching out to place my hand on his shoulder. "You have to fight this. Heaven's army is here to help, but you have to want it and believe you have it. You have to resist them with everything you have!"

Laura was beside herself, tears streaming down her face as she clung to Steven, praying aloud for his deliverance. "God, please, help us. Protect us from this darkness," she pleaded.

The battle seemed to go on forever, the succubus fighting with all its might to maintain its hold on Steven. When things have gotten this bad and gone on this long, it seems like the demons believe that they own the person. Gradually, I could feel the demonic presence beginning to weaken. The oppressive weight in the room started to lift, and the temperature slowly returned to normal. The flickering lights steadied, and the shrieking in Steven's ears began to fade.

With one final, authoritative command, I shouted, "In the name of Jesus Christ, I bind you and cast you out! You have no power here! You will not harm anyone here when you go, but go you will to the feet of Jesus".

The succubus let out a final, furious scream, and then, suddenly, it was gone. The room fell silent, the oppressive atmosphere dissolving into a peaceful calm. Steven sagged in exhaustion, and collapsed into Laura's arms, sobbing uncontrollably, with his body shaking with relief.

For a moment, all was still. The darkness had been driven back, and it seemed as though Steven and Laura had been given a new lease on life. They clung to each other, grateful for the chance to start over, to rebuild what had been broken, but the question was could they cling to their newly awakened faith in God to keep them there.

Ongoing Struggles and Renewed Attacks

In the days and weeks that followed, Steven and Laura began to heal. They attended Christian counseling together, worked on rebuilding their relationship, and strengthening their faith. For a while, it seemed like everything was going to be okay as the nightmares stopped. The oppressive atmosphere in their home had lifted, and

Steven felt a renewed sense of hope and purpose.

But the road to recovery was not an easy one. Steven struggled with guilt and shame over what he had done, and the temptations that had once led him down a dark path still lingered in the back of his mind. He threw himself into his work, making the mistake of worldly feelings. He would not quit his job as he felt it was how he paid his bills and maintained their lifestyle. True faith would have had him depending on God as his provider and left the proximity to sexual deviance behind. He felt that by being aware of the temptations, he would be able to resist and keep himself busy enough to avoid the thoughts that threatened to pull him back into darkness.

That is the problem often with the ego in man. They feel they are in control of things and put their faith in their own processes. It wasn't long before the succubus returned, this time in a more subtle form. Steven began to notice strange occurrences in his daily life as women he had never met before began approaching him in public, offering themselves to him without any provocation. He would be at the grocery store, at a coffee shop, or even just walking down the street, and suddenly, a woman would appear out of nowhere, whispering suggestive comments, tempting him with offers of physical pleasure.

At first, Steven thought it was just a coincidence and his ego felt it was just his natural attractiveness. Yet, as the frequency and intensity of these encounters increased, he realized that the succubus was trying to lure him back into his old habits. It was as if the demon was testing him, probing for any sign of weakness, looking for a way back into his life. Being aware of the tactic, Steven thought he was able to handle things. He was wrong.

The temptations became harder to resist. Steven found himself thinking about the women who had approached him, wondering what it would be like to give in, to let himself be seduced by the darkness once more. He knew he shouldn't be having these thoughts, but the flesh was weak and the allure was strong; the pull almost irresistible.

The Second Deliverance Session

When I received a call from Steven, his voice was shaky and filled with fear. "Russ, I don't know what to do," he admitted. "It's happening again. I feel like I'm losing control, like something is trying to pull me back into the darkness."

I got James involved and had him spend more time with Steven and Laura, but I knew that we needed to act fast. The succubus was obviously not going to give up easily, and it was clear that it had found a way to keep its grip on Steven. I set up a day on the calendar and went back to their home, prepared for another battle.

As soon as I walked through the door, I could feel the oppressive atmosphere that had returned. It was as if the air itself was thick with malevolence, pressing down on everyone inside. Steven looked better than before but his eyes were hollow and dark circles underlining his eyes were more from fear than exhaustion. Laura was by his side as always, her face pale and strained, clearly struggling to keep it together.

We gathered in their living room once again, and I began to pray, asking for God's protection and strength. As I called on the power of Jesus Christ, I could feel the demonic presence pushing back, resisting with everything it had. The succubus attacked more ferociously this time as if it was desperate, knowing the end was near. The whispers grew louder, filling Steven's mind with dark thoughts, telling him that he would never be free, that he was destined to fall back into his old ways. Shadows danced on the floors and walls. The demon seemed more desperate, as if it knew this might be its last chance to hold onto Steven.

I continued to pray, raising my voice above the din of the demonic chaos. "In the name of Jesus Christ, I command you to leave this man and this house! You have no authority here, and you must leave now!"

The battle raged on, and I could feel the tension in the room growing as the succubus fought back with all its might. But I knew we couldn't give up. We had to push through, to fight with everything we had. Finally, as before after a shorter but more intense fight, the succubus let out a final, ear-piercing shriek and then vanished. The room fell silent, and the oppressive atmosphere lifted once more.

A Fragile Peace

For a while, it seemed like things were getting better. Steven was able to transfer to a different, lower classification of prison and no longer had to work with the sex offenders. Steven and Laura continued to attend counseling, and he threw himself into his faith, praying daily for strength and guidance. They worked hard to rebuild their marriage, focusing on open communication and trust. Steven had removed the door from his office and made sure his computer was viewable from the hallway. The nightmares stopped, the temptations lessened, and there was a renewed sense of peace in their home.

But the damage that had been done was not easily undone. Not only in Steven's psyche but also in the marriage. Laura's faith in Steven had been severely wounded by the admissions of his fantasies about wanting her raped and even more so about the plans he made for her sister. Steven still struggled with the shame and guilt over his actions, and the memories of the fantasies that had consumed him were never far from his mind. He did his best to stay strong, but the darkness was always lurking in the background, waiting for an opportunity to return.

The Final Confrontation

Six months after the second deliverance session, Steven and Laura had a heated argument. It was about something trivial, a small misunderstanding that had been blown out of proportion, but the stress of everything they had been through weighed heavily on both of them. The argument escalated quickly, and Steven, feeling overwhelmed and defeated, stormed out of the house.

Desperate for a way to calm his nerves, Steven found himself wandering the streets, lost in thought. Without realizing it, he ended up at a local bar. He ordered a drink, then another, and before he knew it, he was drunk. The succubus, sensing its opportunity, returned with a vengeance. The temptations that Steven had fought so hard to resist flooded back, stronger than ever. He found himself thinking about the women who had approached him, the dark fantasies that had once consumed him, and he felt the familiar pull of the darkness taking hold.

Blinded by alcohol and temptation, Steven made a series of poor decisions that would ultimately lead to his downfall. He left the bar and stumbled into the red-light district, where he was approached by what he thought was a prostitute. In his intoxicated state, he gave in to the succubus's influence and agreed to go with her.

Unbeknownst to Steven, the area was under surveillance due to an ongoing prostitution bust. Upon entering the room, within minutes, he found himself surrounded by police officers and was arrested.

Staring into the darkness

The humiliation and shame of being caught in such a situation was overwhelming, and Steven who thought he had it all under control, knew he had hit rock bottom.

The Aftermath

When Laura found out about Steven's arrest, she was devastated. This was compounded when the bust came out in the newspaper. She had stood by him through so much, but this was the final straw. She couldn't continue to live with the darkness that had taken hold of him, and she knew that their marriage was over. Laura filed for divorce, and Steven was left alone, his life in shambles.

I tried to reach out to Steven after the incident, hoping to offer some guidance and support, but he refused to see me. He was consumed by shame and guilt, unable to face the reality of what his life had become. The succubus had won, and Steven had lost everything.

To this day, Steven has not recovered. He fell deeper into his addiction, his life spiraling further out of control. With the arrest, he lost his job, his family, and his faith, and he now spends his days wandering the streets, lost in darkness.

The story of Steven Matthews is a tragic reminder of the dangers of allowing darkness into our lives.

Chapter 9

A Haunting in the Suburbs

Note: This chapter contains content related to sexual violence that may be distressing for survivors.

The Ghost Hunters' Arrival

It was a late summer evening when the team of ghost hunters arrived at the Anderson family's suburban home. The Andersons had reached out to them after months of strange occurrences that left them terrified and helpless. Objects would move on their own, shadow creatures appeared at random times, and the children had been pushed or assaulted by unseen forces. The family hoped the ghost hunters could provide answers to the unsettling events they had been experiencing.

The team consisted of three seasoned investigators: Jake, a former police officer turned paranormal investigator; Lisa, a medium with years of experience communicating with spirits; and Greg, a tech expert who handled all the equipment and electronics. With years of paranormal experience, they had seen their fair share of strange phenomena and considered themselves well-prepared for any situation. They set up their equipment throughout the house, placing cameras in every room and using EMF detectors to measure any paranormal activity.

Staring into the darkness

After an hour of preparation, the ghost hunters gathered in the living room to begin their investigation. Jake began asking questions, attempting to communicate with whatever entity might be present. "Is there anyone here with us?" he called out, his voice steady and commanding.

Lisa closed her eyes, trying to tune in to the energy around her. She sensed a presence, but it felt different from anything she had encountered before. It was darker, more malevolent. She opened her eyes, worry etched across her face. "I don't think this is a trapped spirit, Jake," she said quietly. "It feels...wrong."

Jake had seen lots of dark and strange things during his years on the force and broke out in a smile. "This could be interesting then. Maybe this could be the one that gets us a TV show, just like we've been talking about"

What had started out as a cool hobby after seeing it on television, had become a time-consuming and sometimes expensive venture. Though Lisa and Greg had other minor revenue streams, Jake was living on his cop's pension and was hoping for a good payday could allow him to live comfortably and travel the country of the world on some studio's dime while yelling at ghosts and getting famous.

Once Greg was done, the team started to walk around the house trying to get something recorded. When they were close to the main bedroom, there was more response to the EMF. Greg and Jake's excitement were quelled by Lisa suddenly grabbing them both in a death grip while trying to stay on her feet. They both grabbed her to keep him from falling.

"What's wrong/", Greg asked worriedly. "You alright".

Lisa had bone white pale and broken out in a sweat. Her eyes had rolled back in her head and she was breathing heavily. As they half supported, half carried Lisa, the EMF detectors started going off wildly. The lights flickered, and a cold breeze swept through the room, causing everyone to shiver.

Lisa suddenly stood straight up and looked at them, but though it was Lisa standing there, it was very different at the same time. Gone was the loving, kind face and laughing eyes. The person looking at them was purely predatory. She smiled at them both and snarled in a voice that definitely was not Lisa's, "Get the fuck out of here and take this stupid bitch with you.".

Jake and Greg were stunned, mouths agape. All they had talked about was getting solid evidence of the paranormal, but time after time it was little to nothing—garbled whispers that could be anything, a glowing orb, EMF spikes, or sudden temperature changes, but nothing like this. With the overwhelming shock came an immediate fight-or-flight response. Jake, who had spent most of his adult life facing dangerous situations, was now afraid all the way to his core. He knew that what was facing him now was more dangerous than anything he had encountered on the streets. Without realizing it, he had involuntarily moved his right hand to where his service weapon would have been, only to clutch empty air.

Even Greg, the biggest skeptic on the team, was visibly shaken.

"Hey, you fucker", he shouted when he was able to find his voice. He had seen Lisa take on other personas many times in their years of working together, but his was nothing like he had seen before. This was primal and violent. It looked like she was ready to attack them both at any second. "Get out of Lisa now. You want to go hard at someone, come at me".

Suddenly, Greg, who had taken a closer step toward Lisa, was lifted off his feet and thrown across the room. He hit the wall with a thud and crumpled to the floor, dazed and disoriented. Lisa had not touched him in any way, but there was no question of who was now in charge and attacking.

Jake who had just watched a two-hundred-and-twenty-pound man tossed like an empty fast-food wrapper, reached out and grabbed Lisa by the arms. She smiled at him, instantly turning his insides to jelly. Lisa grabbed his forearms with her hands and removed his hands where they had been clamped. She pressed them against her chest and laughed.

"Come on Jake, you know you would rather have them there. You've wanted to fuck this stupid whore for months. Maybe before

I let her go, I'll make her blow you", she smiled as whatever was invading Lisa ran her tongue over her lips suggestively. "You'd like that wouldn't you? Or maybe I'll make her fuck you and Greg both at the same time like the slut she is".

Jake was frozen in place, staring that this thing that was Lisa but wasn't as his hands were forced to maul her breasts. In hundreds of violent confrontations over his career, he had never been paralyzed in place or this scared. Scariest of all was the fact that though he outweighed Lisa by at least a hundred pounds and was an avid weightlifter, he couldn't budge the grip on his arms no matter how hard he tried.

The creature in Lisa seemed to get even more amused by his struggles. "Maybe after I'm done fucking you both, I'll take hold you down while I make Greg fuck you in the ass". It laughed a hideous cackle as if it had a vision of this and it was the funniest thing in the world.

It held Jake in place while Greg moaned and tried to get back to his feet. It pulled him closer to Lisa and using her tongue, slowly licked Jake from his chin to his nose. Try as he might, he could not pull away.

"Yum", it purred as it returned Lisa's tongue to her mouth. "You are scrumptious and as fun as it may be to play with you all, I've better things to do. But before I let this slut go, let me be perfectly clear, if you ever come back here and try to interfere with my pets, I will not only do what I said I would do, I'll bite your dick off and spit it in your face when I'm done."

"Do you understand me?", it asked, raising Lisa's eyebrows in a questioning manner.

Barely able to find his voice, Jake stammered, "Yeah, I got you. We are out of here if you let her go. We won't bother you ever again."

The thing in Lisa smiled wickedly, "I almost wish you would. I would have enjoyed making this whore perform for us". Then as quickly as Lisa had become something else, she was back and collapsing on the floor.

Jake bent down to check on her, but as soon as he touched her, she flinched back and screamed. The look she gave Jake was a mix of pure terror and revulsion as she scooted across the floor to put her back against the wall. Greg was just getting over the group as she looked up at them.

"Just don't fucking touch me, okay!", she shouted as she wrapped her arms around herself. "That thing was in me, controlling me! I could see and feel everything but was helpless. This was no earthbound spirit. In all my life, in all the times a spirit has spoken through me, it was not like this. It's usually a tender and consensual thing as I feel it around and allow it in. This was violent and brutal. By the time I felt it near, it was already taking over my mind and body.

As Lisa cried and shook, they could hear a faint laugher seeming to come from the air around them.

Suddenly with a burst of energy, Lisa bound up, almost knocking Jake down in the process. "I'm getting the fuck out of here", she stated as she moved past them at a run. They ran after her, not even bother to gather their equipment.

No one spoke as they jumped I Greg's van and raced out of the driveway and onto the main road. They stayed silent until they were miles down the road and Greg pulled over into an empty parking lot.

"What the fuck was that", Greg screamed looking at his team.

Lisa still would not meet Jake's eyes, recalling the conversation and the visuals the thing had put in her head of her performing lewd acts on them. She simply looked out the passenger window still clutching herself.

"I don't know, but I know I cannot ever do that again. I was raped one night when I was a teenager by boy from school and that was nothing compared to the violation I felt tonight. I had thought that rape was the worst thing a woman could possibly experience. Something so personal, so forcibly taken, but it was just my body. Today, if felt like it was my body and my soul that was raped. I could only exist in a corner of my mind while that thing moved and spoke.

While it forced Jake to manhandle me and sent visions of being forced to perform those things." She was shaking her head violently. "Never again".

"I just hope whatever it was, stays there", Jake stated with a lowered fearful voice.

Panic continued to set in as the team realized they were dealing with something far more dangerous than a simple haunting and knew they were in over their heads. When he had first gotten into ghost hunting, he had heard me speak on a podcast about the dangers and possible confrontations with demonic spirits. Without really believing in these things, he had sent a friend request to my Facebook account, and we had stayed tertiary friends, discussing the supernatural world for a couple of years. Back in their van, Jake pulled out his phone and called me.

The Call for Help

"Russ, we need your help," Jake said, his voice filled with urgency. "We thought we were dealing with a ghost, but this is something much darker. It threw Greg across the room like he was nothing and took over Lisa. You know me. I'm not afraid of shit, but today I was. Whatever that was, it was no more concerned about me than if I was an ant. I was so afraid I literally pissed myself. I don't know what that was, but I think it was a demon, …….no I know it was. Please come help, because we don't know what to do."

I listened carefully, recognizing the fear in Jake's voice. Ghost hunters often encountered spirits, but this was definitely something more. Jake's group had played where they shouldn't have and the warnings I had been giving him for years had materialized. This was a far more dangerous and unpredictable entity than an earthbound spirit. "I'll be there as soon as I can," I assured him. "Tell the family to stay calm and avoid any more contact with whatever is in that house."

I arrived at the Andersons' home later that evening. The family was visibly shaken, especially the children. The mother, Karen, and the father, Mike, were doing their best to keep it together, but the fear in their eyes was unmistakable. Considering the ghost hunter group that had been here had ditched, leaving their equipment and told them they would not be back, it was understandable. After introducing myself, I sat down with them to gather more information about what had been happening.

Karen began to explain the strange occurrences. Her voice trembling. "It started a few months ago. We'd hear noises at night— footsteps, whispers. Then things started moving on their own, and the kids were being pushed and scratched."

Mike added, "Our youngest, Lily, has been talking to an invisible friend she calls 'Mr. Shadow.' At first, we thought it was just her imagination, but then our oldest, Ryan, was teasing her about it, and he was suddenly picked up and slammed against the side of the house. We knew then that something was very wrong, and we had saw the advertisement of the ghost group on Facebook, so we gave them a call".

As they spoke, I noticed three linear scratches on the legs and backs of the children—classic signs of demonic attacks. This was no ordinary haunting; it was a malevolent presence that had targeted the family, particularly the children.

The Investigation Begins

I began my investigation by walking through the house, praying for protection and discernment. The air was heavy with a dark energy that seemed to seep into every corner. As I walked through the living room, I felt a sudden chill, and the hairs on the back of my neck stood up. I knew at once that we were dealing with a powerful demonic force, one that had been given access to this family.

When I returned to the living room, I asked Karen and Mike if there was anything in their lives that could have opened a door to this entity. They seemed to take time thinking about it but could come up with nothing. I told them that it could be the smallest thing or even not something that they had done, but something they had. I went through how generational curses and cursed items could affect people. I was discussing occult activities when they looked at each other nervously before Karen finally spoke up. "I don't know if this has anything to do with it, but I practice Reiki," she admitted. "I've been doing it for years to help people heal. It's supposed to be a good thing, right?"

I felt a pang of concern. Reiki, though often promoted as a healing practice, can sometimes serve as a gateway to spiritual influences that are not from God. "Karen, Reiki can open spiritual doors and can be one of the most dangerous lies that the enemy tells. See, it supposedly does help people, and thus not only does the practitioner keep doing it, but the person who gets the healing often is affected. In fact, it can be so "good" that the person learns it and starts doing it to others also. It's possible that your practice has allowed something dark to enter your home."

Karen shook her head, clearly conflicted. "But I've always used it to help people. It's brought them comfort and healing. How could that be bad?"

I could see the sincerity in her eyes, but I also knew the danger of the path she was on. "Karen, not everything that seems good is from God. The enemy can disguise himself as an angel of light, deceiving people into opening doors that should remain closed. If you want me to help your family, you need to stop practicing Reiki and renounce any connection to it."

She hesitated, her face a mixture of defiance and fear. "I don't know if I can do that. It's a big part of who I am, and I've helped so many people with it."

I sighed, feeling a deep sadness. "Karen, I understand that this is difficult, but I can't help your family if you continue to engage in practices that invite darkness into your home. I'm here to fight for you, but you have to be willing to let go of anything that's giving this entity access."

Despite my warnings, Karen refused to stop her Reiki practice. She was convinced it was a gift from God, and she couldn't understand how it could be the cause of so much suffering. I felt torn, wanting to help the family but knowing that without her willingness to turn away from Reiki, any attempt at deliverance would be futile. I made the difficult decision to leave, telling them to call me if they changed their minds.

A Call for Desperation

A week later, my phone rang again. It was Mike, his voice filled with desperation. "Russ, we need you. Please come back. Ryan was pushed down the stairs last night and broke his collarbone. Karen has agreed to stop practicing Reiki or anything else you ask. We'll do whatever it takes to get rid of this thing."

I arrived at the Andersons' home to find them in a state of fear and chaos. Ryan was sitting on the couch, his arm in a sling, looking pale and shaken. Karen was by his side, tears streaming down her face as she held him close. "I'm so sorry," she whispered. "I never wanted any of this to happen."

I nodded, feeling a glimmer of hope. "Okay, let's start by renouncing any spiritual ties you have to Reiki. We need to close the doors that have been opened and take authority over this house. But before we start, is there anything else that's being held back. If we start this, we will be attacking something that will not take it kindly and will retaliate with a vengeance." I had no idea what it was, but something was telling me I did not have the whole story.

Karen nodded, her resolve firm, so we gathered in the living room, and I led them in a prayer of renunciation, asking God to close any doors that had been opened through her Reiki practice and to remove any demonic influence that had entered their home. As we prayed, I could feel the atmosphere begin to shift, the dark energy in the house starting to dissipate. This was a Christian household, and the name of Jesus cannot be denied. Yet, I the nagging feeling in my soul was even more inflamed by how easy everything seemed.

We continued with a full deliverance session, commanding any demonic presence to leave in the name of Jesus Christ. The house was filled with a sense of peace, and for the first time in weeks, the Andersons felt a sense of hope. They promised to follow up with their pastor and have the children baptized.

A False Peace

For a few days, things seemed to improve. The strange occurrences stopped, and the oppressive atmosphere in the house had lifted. Karen and Mike were grateful, and the children seemed to be returning to their normal selves, but something didn't sit right with me. I couldn't shake the feeling that there was more to this situation, and that I hadn't fully uncovered the truth.

I continued to pray for the family, asking God for discernment and guidance. I knew that if there was any deception or hidden sin, it would only be a matter of time before the darkness returned.

My fears were confirmed a few days later when I received another frantic call from Mike. "Russ, it's happening again. The house is going crazy' appliances are moving, things are breaking, and the lights keep shattering. Please, come back!"

I rushed to the Andersons' home, feeling a sense of dread wash over me. When I arrived, the house was in disarray. The kitchen appliances had been moved across the floor, picture frames were smashed, and the living room lights had been shattered. The sprinkler system kept turning on and off, soaking the house with water.

Karen was sitting on the couch, her face pale and her hands trembling. "I don't understand," she said, her voice barely above a whisper. "I stopped practicing Reiki, just like you said. Why is this happening?"

I could feel the tension in the room, the sense of something being hidden. I turned to Karen, my voice firm. "Are you sure you stopped? Completely?"

She hesitated, her eyes avoiding mine. "Well, I stopped doing it for other people, but...I still practice it for myself. My Angel Guide says it's a gift from God, and that I would be grieving the Holy Spirit to deny it."

My heart sank. I realized then that we were dealing with more than just a simple misunderstanding. Karen had been deceived, and her refusal to fully let go of her practices had left the door wide open for the demonic forces to return.

"Karen, this isn't from God," I said, my voice filled with urgency. "You're being deceived by a demonic entity masquerading as an angel of light. If you continue down this path, you're putting your entire family in danger."

She shook her head, tears streaming down her face. "I can't believe that. I've felt so much peace and love from my Angel Guide. People have been healed from some seriously traumatic illnesses from this. Even the Bible talks about laying on of hands for healing. That's all I'm doing. How could that be wrong?" This is something that truly angered me about the church. The Christian church does not speak about these occult practices or demonic attacks. Sermons tend to tickle the ears and preach about life's lessons, but not the great commission. They don't train spiritual warriors or even prepare everyday believers for the dangers around them.

I sighed, feeling a deep sadness for the family. "Karen, I can't force you to believe me, but I'm telling you the truth. If you don't stop, if you don't fully renounce this, I can't help you. The attacks will continue, and they will only get worse."

Karen refused to listen, convinced that her angel guide was a gift from God. I knew then that my hands were tied. I couldn't perform another deliverance session if she wasn't willing to truly repent and turn away from her practices.

Deliverance is not a magical forcefield that disperses demons and keeps people safe. It is a change in life; it is a repentance of past sins and a commitment to living a life for God. With no repentance, there is no protection.

Tragedy Strikes

A week later, tragedy struck. Ryan, the oldest son, had fallen from a tree while playing with his siblings. Ryan's sister said everything was fine until he had grabbed for a branch to pull himself higher only to miss the branch and fall. He had hit is head and was taken to the hospital unresponsive. Despite the doctors' best efforts, his condition deteriorated quickly and within 48 hours, he was dead. She said she was sure the branch had moved when he grabbed for it.

The news hit me hard, and I felt a deep sense of guilt and sorrow, knowing that I had failed to protect this family. I had allowed myself to be convinced that Karen was sincere in her desire to change, but her deception had cost her son his life. The weight of that realization was almost too much to bear.

I attended Ryan's funeral, my heart heavy with grief. I could see the pain etched into Karen's face, the realization of what her actions had brought upon her family. She had lost her son because she had refused to let go of something that she believed was good, but that had ultimately brought destruction. As I stood at the graveside, I prayed for Ryan's soul and for the healing of the Anderson family. I prayed for Karen, that she would see the truth and turn away from the darkness that had ensnared her. But I also prayed for myself, asking God to forgive me for my part in this tragedy though I had no idea what I could have done differently.

The Weight of Guilt

The guilt of what happened to the Andersons has stayed with me to this day. I have carried the weight of Ryan's death, knowing that I should have been more discerning, and that I should have walked away when I realized Karen wasn't fully committed to changing her ways. Sadly, this would not be the last weight that would settle on my conscious during my ministry. There would be another that would almost push me past my breaking point.

The demonic forces continue to bring up this failure in my

deliverance meetings, taunting me with the memory of Ryan's death, trying to shake my faith and undermine my confidence. But I have learned that even in the face of failure and loss, God's grace is sufficient. I have learned to lean on Him for strength and guidance, trusting that He can bring healing even in the darkest of circumstances.

Sadly, I cannot report a happy ending to this tale. Karen, bereft with grief over what happened refused to be consoled over Ryan's death. Mike was no help as he also blamed her and this ultimately led to the destruction of their marriage. I pray for Karen's soul as she committed suicide from prescription medication less than a year later. The despicable creatures had blasphemed healing and only brought death and destruction. Mike moved the rest of the family away and cut ties with the past.

And so, I continue to fight against the forces of darkness, knowing that I must be vigilant and discerning, always listening for the voice of the Holy Spirit and trusting in His power to bring deliverance and healing to those who are willing to turn away from the darkness and embrace the light.

The story of the Andersons serves as a sobering reminder of the dangers of opening spiritual doors without fully understanding the consequences. It reminds me that not everything that seems good is from God, and that we must always be on guard against the deceptions of the enemy. As I move forward in my ministry, I carry the memory of Ryan and Karen with me, a constant reminder of the importance of discernment and the need for true repentance. And I pray that the Andersons, wherever they are, have found peace and healing in the arms of our Savior.

Chapter 10

A Dangerous Playmate

Introduction to Pastor Daniel's Family

Pastor Daniel Peterson was a devoted man of God, known for his heartfelt sermons and compassionate nature. He had served his congregation faithfully and though only recently in position, always put his flock's needs above his own. I had been a friend of Daniels predecessor at the church. In fact, it was this same predecessor who suggested I speak to the Assembly of God Church where I pastored for years. Daniel lived in the parsonage next to the church with his wife, Sarah, and their two children, eight-year-old Lily and twelve-year-old Michael. To those who knew them, they seemed like the perfect family—happy, close-knit, and deeply rooted in their faith.

But in recent months, Daniel had noticed some unsettling changes in his youngest daughter, Lily. It started innocently enough, or so he thought. Lily had begun talking about an imaginary friend named "Mira." At first, Daniel and Sarah didn't think much of it. Many children create imaginary friends, especially at Lily's age. They assumed it was just a phase, a harmless game that she would eventually outgrow. This is once again, one of the dangerous games evil plays. This is a common theme I have seen played over dozens of times in my ministry, yet it was not something covered in seminary or Bible college. I've been to school at one of the most conservative bible colleges in the nation. There is little to nothing taught about spiritual warfare of the attacks of the enemy in the real world. Daniel was a seasoned pastor, yet did not see the darkness happening in his own home.

However, as weeks turned into months, Mira seemed to take on a life of her own, and Lily's behavior began to change. She became more secretive, more defiant, and started getting into trouble both at home and at school. Whenever she was caught misbehaving, she would blame Mira, saying that her friend told her to do it. At first, Daniel thought it was just a way for Lily to avoid responsibility, but the situation quickly escalated, becoming more than just a childhood game.

The Imaginary Friend

It began with small incidents that were easy to dismiss. Lily would act out in minor ways, like drawing on the walls with crayons or sneaking cookies from the kitchen late at night. When confronted, she would insist, "It wasn't me, Daddy. It was Mira! She made me do it!" Daniel and Sarah tried to be patient, gently correcting her and explaining that Mira wasn't real, that she needed to take responsibility for her actions.

But Lily's behavior continued to worsen. She started lying, not just about small things, but about serious matters. She accused her older brother, Michael, of taking things from her room, and when they confronted Michael, he denied it vehemently. The accusations escalated into full-blown fights between the siblings, with Lily screaming at Michael to stay away from her and Mira.

Then, things started disappearing around the house—small, everyday items like spoons, scissors, and pieces of jewelry. They would search high and low, only to find them hidden in Lily's room, tucked away in strange places like under her mattress or inside her toy chest. Each time, Lily would tearfully insist that Mira had taken them, and that she wasn't to blame.

The situation came to a head one afternoon when Daniel found Lily sitting in her room, crying softly. He immediately went to her side, wrapping his arms around her and asking what was wrong.

"Mira is mad at me," Lily sobbed, her little body shaking with fear. "She says I have to hurt my friends, or she won't be my friend anymore."

Daniel's heart sank. This was more than just a game; this was something darker. He had seen enough in his years as a pastor to know when a situation was serious, and this felt serious. He held Lily close, whispering words of comfort, but inside, he felt a growing sense of dread. He knew he needed to do something, but he was torn. How could his daughter, in their own home, the parsonage, be under demonic influence?

The Growing Fear

Daniel spent the next few days in deep prayer, asking God for wisdom and guidance. He tried to talk to Lily, to understand more about Mira, but every time he brought it up, she would shut down, refusing to speak. She seemed frightened, not just of Mira, but of something she couldn't quite articulate.

Sarah, too, was growing increasingly concerned. She had noticed changes in Lily's behavior—how she would sometimes stare off into space as if listening to someone who wasn't there, or how she would suddenly burst into tears for no apparent reason. There was a darkness that seemed to be settling over their home, an unseen presence that was slowly but surely taking hold of their daughter.

One night, Daniel woke up to the sound of Lily screaming. He and Sarah rushed to her room to find her standing in the middle of her bed, pointing to the corner of the room and shouting, "Go away! Leave me alone!" Her eyes were wide with terror, and her face was pale and drawn.

"What's wrong, sweetheart?" Sarah asked, trying to calm her down.

"It's Mira!" Lily cried. "She's mad at me! She says I have to do what she says, or she'll hurt you!"

Daniel and Sarah exchanged a worried glance. This was beyond their experience; beyond anything they had ever dealt with before.

They were at a loss for what to do.

Daniel tried to reassure Lily, telling her that Mira wasn't real, that she couldn't hurt anyone. But even as he said the words, he felt a nagging doubt in the back of his mind. Something about this felt too real, too dangerous to ignore.

A Call for Help

As the days went on, the situation continued to deteriorate. Lily's behavior became more erratic, more aggressive. She would lash out at her parents and her brother, screaming and throwing things whenever they tried to talk to her about Mira. She became increasingly withdrawn, spending hours alone in her room, refusing to eat or come out.

Daniel knew he needed help, but he didn't know where to turn. As a pastor, he was supposed to be the one providing guidance and support, not the one asking for it. He felt ashamed, embarrassed that he couldn't figure out how to better parent his daughter. It was a "physician heal thyself" situation as he would speak to others about raising children according to God's word.

He was speaking to Tony, his predecessor, about Lily acting up when Tony asked if he had tried praying over her. Daniel answered that, of course, he had prayed about it. Tony stopped him and stated, "Not prayed for, but over." He also asked if the parsonage had been blessed again between the time he had moved out and Daniel had moved in.

Daniel was confused, to say the least. "I don't understand. Why would the parsonage need to be blessed? It's on church property and the house of the pastor."

Tony had worked with me in the past, and I had attended his church many times. He then told Daniel about a deliverance minister who lived not far and suggested he should give me a call. Daniel laughed it off at first. "A deliverance minister? I don't even know what that is, to be honest."

Tony explained what a deliverance minister was and how we had worked together in the past. Daniel still seemed incredulous.

"You mean like those Vatican priests they call in when people are possessed? "You think my daughter's possessed by demons", Daniel asked with a little anger going into his voice.

"No", Tony explained. "I don't think she is possessed. I do know that demons attack pastors and their families often. I did not understand until Russ explained it to me. How many do you know that leave their calling after marriage troubles, family issues, infidelity, alcoholism, etc. And these were people you never would have thought had any issues. It was like a slap in the face when Russ had me actually think about it. What better way to attack a church than derail its leader?".

Staring into the darkness

I had shared stories of my work, of the battles fought against demonic forces, and more than a few had been from attacks on clergy. Daniel, who had been incredulous was struck by sincerity in Tony's voice. Maybe this Russ could help them, could offer some insight into what was happening to Lily.

With a heavy heart, Daniel thanked Tony and picked up the phone and called me, explaining the situation as best he could. I listened carefully, asking questions and taking notes. When Daniel finished, there was a long silence on the other end of the line.

"Daniel," I finally said, my voice calm and steady, "I'm going to come out there and see what's going on. It sounds like you're dealing with something serious, and I want to help in any way I can."

The Toy with a Dark Secret

I arrived at the parsonage the next morning, a sense of urgency in my step. As I stepped into the house, I could feel the heavy, oppressive atmosphere that seemed to hang in the air. It was like walking into a fog of darkness, thick and suffocating. This was not the happy, peaceful parsonage I have visited so many times in my past.

Daniel greeted him at the door, his face etched with worry and exhaustion. "Thank you for coming, Russ," he said, his voice barely above a whisper. "I don't know what to do. I've prayed, I've tried everything, but nothing seems to help."

I nodded, placing a reassuring hand on Daniel's shoulder. "We'll figure this out together," I said. "Why don't you show me Lily's room?"

We made our way down the hall, passing by Michael, who was sitting at the kitchen table, his head buried in his hands. Sarah was in the living room, her eyes red and swollen from crying. The whole family seemed to be on the edge, hanging by a thread.

When they reached Lily's room, I immediately felt a surge of dark energy. The room was cold, colder than the rest of the house, and there was a strange smell in the air, like something rotten and decaying. Not strong as in many cases, but like an underlying smell as if something had been put in a trashcan and gone bad.

Lily was sitting on her bed, clutching a stuffed bear to her chest, her eyes wide and filled with fear. She looked up as I entered, her expression wary and uncertain.

"Hi, Lily," I said softly, kneeling to her level. "I'm Pastor Russ. Your dad asked me to come and talk to you."

Lily didn't say anything, just stared at me with a haunted look in her eyes. I could see the fear, the confusion, and she had the look of someone being trapped by something she didn't understand.

As I spoke to Lily, I noticed she clutched the bear even tighter, shielding it from me.

"Lily," I said gently, pointing to the bear, "can you tell me about this? Where did you get it?"

Lily glanced at the doll, her expression darkening. "Mira gave it to me," she said, her voice barely above a whisper. "She said it was her favorite."

I exchanged a glance with Daniel, his concern growing. "Do you know where Mira got it?"

Lily shook her head. "No. She just brought it with her one day. She said it was special."

Daniel looked puzzled. "That bear? It was left with other items for us when we moved in. Most of the time when we start at a new church, members just donate items to help us set up. This bear was sitting on the front porch with other boxes that were donated.

I frowned, my suspicion deepening. "I think this might be more than just a toy," I said. "I've seen things like this before—objects that have been used in rituals, that carry a dark presence with them. It's possible that this bear is what's been causing all of this. Occult groups do this intentionally. An outright attack, you could defend against or even get authorities involved, but something like this causes rot from within."

The Attack on the Parsonage

As Daniel and I spoke, the temperature in the room suddenly

dropped even further, and a gust of icy wind blew through the house, slamming the doors shut with a loud bang. Lilly pulled the bear closer.

A low, guttural growl echoed through the room, a sound that sent chills down my spine. I could feel the dark spirit in the room, and it was not happy.

"Get the family together," I said urgently, my eyes scanning the room for any sign of movement. "We need to pray, now."

Daniel nodded, rushing out of the room to gather Sarah and Michael. I stayed with Lily, my heart pounding as I felt the demonic presence grow stronger.

As they regrouped in the living room, shadows seemed to move, to twist and writhe like living things. The air was thick with tension, and I could feel the darkness pressing in, trying to break our resolve.

"Everyone, hold hands," I instructed, my voice steady but firm. "We're going to pray together, and we're not going to let this thing have any power over us."

As we began to pray, the room erupted in chaos. The shadows grew darker, more solid, forming twisted, nightmarish shapes that loomed over us. I had the children close their eyes.

The growling grew louder, more menacing, and I could feel the demonic presence pushing back, trying to break their unity, to sow fear and doubt in their hearts. I could see Lily trembling, clutching her mother's hand, her eyes wide with terror.

"Stay strong!" I shouted over the noise, my voice filled with authority. "In the name of Jesus Christ, I command you to leave this house! You have no power here! Daniel and Sarah, you have authority here. Demand it to leave!"

The demon howled in rage, the sound so loud it felt like it could shatter the windows. The shadows seemed to surge forward, wrapping around them like a suffocating blanket, but we didn't relent.

"We rebuke you in Jesus's name!" Daniel and Sarah shouted; their voices filled with conviction. "You have no authority here! Leave our family alone!"

A Family Torn Apart

After what felt like an eternity, the demonic presence finally began to weaken. The shadows slowly receded, the room growing still as the oppressive atmosphere lifted. The growling stopped, leaving the family standing in the middle of the room, shaken but unharmed.

I let out a sigh of relief, my heart still racing. "It's gone for now," I said, turning to Daniel. "But this isn't over. That doll needs to be destroyed, and you need to be vigilant. This thing will try to come back."

Daniel nodded, his face pale but determined. "We'll do whatever it takes. Thank you, Russ."

I smiled, placing a reassuring hand on Daniel's shoulder. "You did well, Daniel. Just remember, God's power is greater than anything these demons can throw at you. Keep your faith strong, and you'll be fine."

Over the next few days, I helped the family destroy the doll and cleanse their home, praying over each room and asking God to remove any remaining darkness. The oppression had been lifted, and Lily began to return to her old self, her fear slowly fading as the days went by.

But the peace didn't last. Word of what had happened at the parsonage quickly spread through the church, and soon, rumors began to circulate. Some members of the congregation were supportive, understanding that the pastor and his family had been under spiritual attack. But others were less forgiving, whispering that Daniel had brought this upon himself, that his faith wasn't strong enough, that a true man of God wouldn't have let this happen.

The whispers grew louder, the rumors more vicious, and soon, Daniel found himself under scrutiny from the church's leadership. They questioned his ability to lead, to protect his flock, and before long, they asked him to step down as pastor.

Daniel was devastated. He had dedicated his life to serving his church, to helping others, and now, he was being cast out because of something he had no control over. He and his family were forced to leave the parsonage, to find a new place to live, a new church to call home.

As I helped them pack up their belongings, Lily clung to her father, tears streaming down her face. "I'm sorry, Daddy," she whispered, her voice filled with guilt. "This is all my fault."

Daniel hugged her tightly, his heart breaking. "No, sweetheart," he said softly. "This isn't your fault. None of this is your fault. We're going to be okay. God has a plan for us, and we're going to trust in Him, no matter what."

A New Beginning

Despite the pain of leaving their home and church behind, Daniel and his family found strength in their faith and in each other. They moved to a new town, where Daniel found a small church that welcomed them with open arms. It wasn't the same, but it was a fresh start, a chance to heal and move forward.

I kept in touch with Daniel, offering support and encouragement as they adjusted to their new life. He knew that the journey ahead wouldn't be easy, but he also knew that God was with them, guiding them every step of the way. In time, the wounds began to heal.

Lily grew stronger, her fear fading as she found solace in her new church and in the love of her family. Michael, too, found new friends and a renewed sense of purpose, and Sarah and Daniel rebuilt their life together, their bond stronger than ever.

Though the experience had been traumatic, it had also taught them valuable lessons about faith, resilience, and the power of God's love. They had faced darkness head-on and emerged stronger, more united, and more determined to stand firm in their faith, no matter what challenges lay ahead. Daniel has become a true warrior in the spiritual battle we have been called to wage. The strongest of weapons are forged by fire to keep them from breaking and Daniels family survived their time in the forge.

Chapter 11

The Dark Reality of Satanic Ritual Abuse

Introduction to Satanic Ritual Abuse

Satanic ritual abuse (SRA) is a deeply disturbing and often hidden practice that involves the systematic abuse and torture of individuals, typically children, within a context of satanic worship. It is a topic that many find hard to believe, often dismissed as conspiracy or hysteria. However, as a deliverance minister, I have encountered more than my fair share of cases involving SRA, and I can attest to its horrifying reality.

SRA is not just a figment of overactive imaginations or urban legends; it is a pervasive evil that lurks in the shadows of society. Those involved in these rituals believe they are harnessing dark powers through their heinous acts, seeking to invoke demonic entities to gain control, power, or other sinister desires. The abuse often includes physical, sexual, and psychological torture, aimed at breaking down the victim's mind and spirit to create a sense of total domination.

This chapter aims to shed light on the reality of SRA, its signs and symptoms, and the profound impact it has on its victims. This dark practice is not the action of demonic hoards that wait for open doors to attack those the walk too far from God's grace, but the neighbors next door, the police chief, and possible the local pastor. These groups are organized and embedded in our everyday world. It is a stark reminder that evil is not just an abstract concept but a very real force that can manifest in the most horrific ways.

The Dangers of Satanic Ritual Abuse

SRA is particularly insidious because it often occurs in secret, hidden behind the façade of normalcy. Perpetrators can be anyone including trusted members of the community, neighbors, teachers, or even family members. The secrecy surrounding these practices is maintained through threats, intimidation, and mind control, ensuring that victims remain silent.

Victims of SRA are subjected to unimaginable horrors. They are often drugged, beaten, sexually assaulted, and forced to participate in rituals that involve blood sacrifices and other macabre practices. Psychological manipulation is intense, as abusers use fear tactics, isolation, and brainwashing to control their victims where the goal is to shatter the victim's sense of reality and instill a deep fear of their abusers, making it nearly impossible for them to seek help or escape. The spiritual damage caused by SRA is profound. Victims are often forced to partake in satanic rites and rituals, which can open doors to demonic oppression or possession. This spiritual bondage is a direct result of the trauma and the satanic acts forced upon the victim, creating a spiritual stronghold that is difficult to break.

In my experience, those who suffer from SRA often display signs of severe trauma, including dissociative identity disorder (formerly known as multiple personality disorder), post-traumatic stress disorder (PTSD), depression, anxiety, and other mental health issues. The abuse can lead to long-lasting emotional scars, and without proper intervention, victims may struggle to reclaim their lives.

Case Study: A Survivor's Story

To illustrate the horrors of SRA, let me share the story of Karen, a woman who came to me for help several years ago. Karen's case is one of the most harrowing I've encountered, and it serves as a powerful example of the dangers of SRA. If you have PTSD from a sexual abuse past, I suggest you skip this chapter as it will be almost as terrible to read as it was to listen to and no write.

Karen grew up in a small town, in a family that appeared normal from the outside, with her father was a respected businessman, and her mother was active in the community. But behind closed doors, Karen's life was a living nightmare. Her parents were heavily involved in a satanic cult, and from a young age, Karen was subjected to horrific abuse as part of the cult's rituals.

The abuse began when Karen was just four years old. She was taken to secret meetings held in dark basements and remote locations, where she witnessed and experienced things no child should ever endure. The rituals were brutal and sadistic, often involving animal sacrifices, chanting, and dark invocations. Karen was forced to participate in these rituals, her small hands guided by her parents to perform unspeakable acts.

As she grew older, the abuse escalated as she was drugged, raped, and beaten with her body used as a vessel for the cult's sick desires. The psychological torment was equally severe. Her parents and other cult members used fear and manipulation to keep her compliant, telling her that if she ever spoke out, she would be killed, and her soul would be damned for eternity. She was also guilt ridden as they forced her hands to commit heinous acts and convinced her that she was just as guilty as they were.

To cope with the abuse, and with full intention by the perpetrators Karen developed dissociative identity disorder. Her mind fragmented into different personalities primarily intended to participate in rituals, each one created to handle the trauma she could not bear. These alters, as they are called, helped her survive, but they also made her feel disconnected from reality. Karen often lost time, finding herself in strange places with no memory of how she got there. Despite the constant fear and pain, Karen managed to escape the cult when she was in her early twenties. She moved to a new city, changed her name, and tried to start a new life. But the memories of the abuse haunted her, and she struggled with severe depression, anxiety, and PTSD.

When Karen came to me, she was desperate for help. She had been experiencing night terrors, seeing dark figures in her home, and feeling an overwhelming sense of dread. She believed that the cult was still watching her, and she was terrified that they would find her and drag her back into their world.

I knew that Karen needed more than just prayer; she needed full deliverance and psychological treatment. I referred to James for treatment as he was also aware of the dark world that I would be working on from the other side. Where normal deliverance removes cancerous growth, SRA situations are more like nerve surgery. There are so many areas where the wrong step at the wrong time can cause things to come crashing down. It would be like tip toeing threw a minefield as each new thing found would either be dealt by me on the spiritual realm or James on the mental. The spiritual strongholds created by the years of abuse were deeply ingrained, and breaking them would require time, patience, and a great deal of spiritual warfare. The mental strongholds created by Karen could only be brought down through the healing of our Lord Jesus and the wonderful skills of James.

The Deliverance Process

The deliverance process with Karen was one of the most challenging and intense I've ever experienced. The demons that had taken hold of her were deeply rooted, their grip on her soul strong and unyielding. They had been given legal rights through the rituals and the abuse she had suffered, and they were not going to let go easily.

I will not be going into details as much in this case as I have in others as it lasted quite some time and Karen is still receiving psychological sessions. Also, the details that were brought out during repentance and interview should never be put in print. I have tears in my eyes even now writing this down recalling the horrors this child of God endured and knowing that others still suffer through it today.

During our first session, Karen sat across from me, her body trembling with fear. The majority of the time we spoke about Jesus and the healing powers of the Holy Spirit and about that God is waiting to heal her whenever she is ready. She was so scared as she lived in fear that the group was going to find her and if they knew about her coming to me, they would hurt James and me. She was worried about them coming after my family and anyone connected to us. I did my best to assure her and convince her were safe. The closes analogy I can give is that of a severely beaten and abused animal. Constantly waiting for the strike to come and unaware of what to do when it doesn't. There was great resistance to attempts to pray and aversion to objects. It was on one of our sessions that her eyes rolled back in her head, and a deep, guttural voice emerged from her lips. "She belongs to us," the demon growled. "You cannot save her. This soul was bought and paid for long ago. Are you deaf or just stupid? Weren't you listening to what she did?"

I could feel the darkness in the room, the oppressive weight of the demonic presence pressing down on us. But this is what I had been waiting for. The demons had not made their presence known before because they had felt assured in their hold. With the trust she was starting to show in James and the inner healing she was starting to accept, they were not so sure anymore. They felt threatened and had come forward to try to intimidate and lie their way out. I knew that we had to press on, that we had to fight for Karen's freedom. "In the name of Jesus Christ, I command you to leave her," I said firmly. "You have no power here, and you must go."

The demon laughed in contempt, its voice echoing through the room. Karen's body convulsed, and she began to cry out in pain, her hands clawing at her throat as if she were being strangled. I continued to pray, calling on the power of Christ to break the chains that bound her. These were old chains. Chains of blood, death, pain, and abuse. The saddest part is these are the hardest chains to break, not because they are made by the powers of darkness, but by the victim. They have built these chains through the lies, pain and abuse of the victim.

The battle was intense, and at times it felt like we were losing. The hardest part of this type of deliverance is convincing the person to accept the healing that Jesus has ready for them. They are so convinced in the very core of their being that they are evil, that they are not worthy of the healing waiting for them. But gradually, with the groundwork lain through weeks of work, Karen was able to believe that God could love even someone like her and that He not only loved here but wanted her to be His child to live with him forever. That only if she let Him, He would wipe the tears away and make her new. On that day, Karen repented of her past and accepted the Lord Jesus into her life. Now this is not some magic phrase and Karen did not have some new almighty faith where she totally believed all that I had told her, but all she needed was a mustard seed and that day she found it. I could feel the demonic presence beginning to weaken. The darkness in the room started to lift, and Karen's body relaxed, her breathing becoming steady and calm.

Over the next few months, we continued the deliverance process and James met with her, each session bringing Karen closer to freedom. The demons fought back with everything they had, trying to maintain their hold on her, but we pressed on, refusing to give in to fear. She was paired up with one of the best partners in Christ as a pastor that I had ever worked with to disciple her along.

Karen's journey to healing was long and difficult, but eventually, she found her way out of the darkness. She began to reclaim her life, to reconnect with the parts of herself that had been lost to the abuse. She found solace in her faith, and with time, she was able to completely forgive her parents and the others who had hurt her.

Staring into the darkness

Today, Karen is a survivor. She has dedicated her life to helping others who have suffered from abuse, using her own experience to bring hope and healing to those who feel lost and broken.

The Reality of SRA in Society

Karen's story is not unique. There are countless others who have suffered from SRA, their stories hidden in the shadows, their voices silenced by fear and shame. SRA is not confined to one area or group; it is a widespread problem that can be found in every corner of society.

The perpetrators of SRA often operate in secret, using their positions of power and influence to hide their activities. They prey on the vulnerable, exploiting their fears and insecurities to maintain control. The victims are often children, chosen because they are easy to manipulate and unlikely to be believed if they speak out.

The secrecy surrounding SRA makes it difficult to quantify its prevalence, but there is no doubt that it is a significant and ongoing issue. Many survivors have come forward in recent years, sharing their stories and shedding light on the dark reality of satanic ritual abuse.

Signs and Symptoms of SRA

Recognizing the signs and symptoms of SRA is crucial for those who work with survivors. The trauma experienced by victims of

SRA is often severe, and the effects can be long-lasting. Here are some common signs and symptoms to look out for:

1. **Dissociative Identity Disorder (DID)**: Many SRA survivors develop DID as a coping mechanism to deal with the trauma. They may have multiple personalities, each one created to handle different aspects of the abuse. Survivors may experience blackouts, lose time, or find themselves in strange places with no memory of how they got there.

2. **Nightmares and Flashbacks**: SRA survivors often experience vivid nightmares and flashbacks of the abuse. These can be triggered by certain sounds, smells, or sights, and can cause intense fear and anxiety.

3. **Self-Harm and Suicidal Ideation**: The psychological trauma of SRA can lead to self-harm and suicidal thoughts. Survivors may feel a deep sense of hopelessness and despair, believing that they will never escape the darkness.

4. **Phobias and Panic Attacks**: Many survivors develop phobias and panic attacks related to the abuse. They may be afraid of certain places, people, or objects that remind them of the rituals.

5. **Trust Issues and Relationship Problems**: SRA survivors often struggle with trust issues and have difficulty forming healthy relationships. They may feel betrayed by those who

were supposed to protect them and may struggle to connect with others on an emotional level.

6. **Spiritual Struggles**: The spiritual damage caused by SRA can be profound. Survivors may feel a deep sense of guilt or shame, believing that they are beyond redemption. They may struggle with their faith, feeling abandoned by God or questioning His existence.

Many times, it doesn't show up looking like SRA. A person may have DID and believe their parent or parents friend molested them or did videos of them. Then as the session progresses, maybe a year into it, identities start surfacing who are very young in age, are like 3 or 4 years old and describe men in hoods, or grandpa with men in hoods coming into their bedroom late at night.

The Role of the Church and Deliverance Ministry

The Church has a critical role to play in addressing SRA. It is essential for the Church to provide a safe and supportive environment for survivors, offering them the love, compassion, and understanding they need to heal.

Deliverance ministry is a vital part of the healing process for many SRA survivors. By breaking the spiritual strongholds created by the abuse, deliverance can help survivors find freedom from the demonic influences that have taken hold of their lives. However, deliverance is not a quick fix; it requires time, patience, and a deep commitment to the healing process and sadly too many in this field are in it for the flash and quick fame and have made a mockery of the ministry and the healing needed.

As a deliverance minister, I have seen firsthand the power of Christ to bring healing and restoration to those who have suffered from SRA. I have witnessed the miraculous transformation of lives that were once consumed by darkness, now filled with hope and light. But I have also seen the devastation wrought by those who can't check their ego's and cause more damage than good.

Preventing SRA

Preventing SRA requires a collective effort from society as a whole. Awareness and education are key components in preventing abuse and protecting vulnerable individuals. Here are some steps that can be taken to help prevent SRA:

1. **Education**: Educating the public about the reality of SRA and the signs to look out for can help identify and prevent abuse. Awareness campaigns, seminars, and workshops can provide valuable information to parents, educators, and community leaders.

2. **Support for Survivors**: Providing support and resources for survivors is crucial in helping them heal and rebuild their lives. Support groups, counseling services, and safe houses can offer survivors the care and protection they need.

3. **Stronger Laws and Enforcement**: Enforcing stronger laws and penalties for those involved in SRA can help deter potential perpetrators. Law enforcement agencies should be trained to recognize the signs of SRA and to investigate cases thoroughly.

4. **Encouraging Open Communication**: Creating an environment where children feel safe to speak out about abuse is vital in preventing SRA. Encouraging open communication and building trust with children can help them feel comfortable sharing their experiences.

Conclusion

Satanic ritual abuse is a dark and terrifying reality that continues to affect countless individuals around the world. It is a reminder that evil is not just an abstract concept but a very real force that can manifest in the most horrific ways. As a society, we must work together to raise awareness, provide support for survivors, and prevent future abuse. The Church has a crucial role to play in this effort, offering love, compassion, and deliverance to those who have been affected by SRA.

In my work as a deliverance minister, I have seen the power of Christ to bring healing and restoration to those who have suffered from SRA. It is my hope that by sharing these stories and raising awareness, we can help bring an end to this horrific practice and offer hope and healing to those who have been affected. My dealings with SRA were earlier in my ministry before I even realized what it truly was. Even with my decades of experience, I will try to refer any case I get involved in this to true experts that do this on a regular basis. SRA goes to a much deeper level than I am comfortable doing as it deals not just with demonic attackers but with living, breathing people. I related to one such expert once that I cannot do this ministry as I am not strong enough. They hear the confessions of these lost souls of how they were repeated sexually and mentally abused for years, often by the same people that were supposed to protect them.

God's word says, "vengeance is mine sayeth the Lord", but a little girl telling me of how her uncle and his friends (women and men) abused her, would only end with me grabbing the closest baseball bat. That is the world's way of handling it and not the proper way for the child's well-being. This is why I stay in my lane of deliverance and just tackle the easy cases where the only things I deal with have already been found guilty by my Lord Jesus and its game on. Pride in this case will only lead to a fall and the demonic are sitting, just waiting for the door to open. If you suspect someone is a victim or you yourself is a victim of SRA, please see an expert. The best SRA expert I know suggests finding a Christian counselor who understands DID inner healing. Beware of finding SRA groups on the internet as most are charlatans or can be ran or infiltrated by

SRA cults.

Final Chapter

Reflections on the Journey of Deliverance

As I reflect on the cases and experiences detailed throughout this book, I am struck by the enduring truth of spiritual warfare and the unshakable power of Christ in the face of evil. The journey of deliverance ministry is not one that can be easily defined or contained within simple terms. It is complex, layered, and often deeply personal. But one thing remains clear: freedom is possible through faith, persistence, and a reliance on God's power.

The Reality of Spiritual Warfare

In today's world, the idea of spiritual warfare is often misunderstood or dismissed. Many people struggle to accept that the spiritual realm can have such a profound impact on their daily lives. However, as seen in the case files and personal stories shared in this book, the effects of demonic oppression, infestation, and possession are very real. The spiritual attacks described are not figments of imagination or exaggerations; they are evidence of a battle that rages beyond the physical, manifesting in very real torment and suffering.

Deliverance ministry is not about fear or glorifying the power of darkness; it is about standing firm in the authority given to us through Jesus Christ. The Bible reminds us that "our struggle is not against flesh and blood, but against the rulers, against the authorities, against the powers of this dark world and against the spiritual forces of evil in the heavenly realms" (Ephesians 6:12). This truth compels us to take action—not out of fear, but out of love and a desire to see people set free.

Faith, Forgiveness, and Freedom

One of the recurring themes throughout the cases is the incredible power of forgiveness, both of self and of others. Many of the individuals who sought deliverance had experienced deep wounds from their past—trauma, abuse, rejection—that opened doors to the enemy. In these cases, the first step toward deliverance often involved the healing of their hearts, through the act of forgiveness. Susan, in particular, struggled with the guilt and shame of past decisions, believing that she was beyond redemption. Her journey shows us that God's grace is infinite, and no one is ever too far gone for His love to reach.

Forgiveness is a key to unlocking the chains that bind us. Jesus Himself taught us to forgive those who have wronged us, knowing that unforgiveness keeps us trapped in a prison of bitterness. As I've seen time and time again, deliverance is not just about casting out demons—it is about restoring hearts to the truth of God's love and healing the wounds that allowed the enemy in.

The Role of Mental Health in Deliverance

Throughout my years in deliverance ministry, I've learned the critical importance of discerning the difference between spiritual and mental health issues. There is no shame in seeking help from professionals, and I have often worked alongside therapists and counselors to ensure that individuals receive the holistic care they need. Deliverance is not a replacement for mental health care; rather, it complements it when the root cause is spiritual in nature.

Kyle's case serves as a reminder of this delicate balance. His symptoms, initially thought to be purely psychological, were later revealed to have spiritual underpinnings. However, this did not negate the need for ongoing counseling and support for his mental health. The integration of spiritual discernment and professional mental health care can lead to profound, lasting freedom. As ministers of deliverance, we must always be humble enough to acknowledge when help is needed from other disciplines and work collaboratively to bring healing.

The Power of Community

Another critical aspect of deliverance ministry that should not be overlooked is the power of community. In several of the cases, individuals found freedom only after they were supported by a strong community of believers—whether it was their church, their family, or a small group of trusted friends. Deliverance is often a process, not a one-time event, and the road to complete healing can be long and difficult.

Isolation, in many cases, is where the enemy thrives. The more isolated a person is—whether physically, emotionally, or spiritually—the easier it is for the enemy to whisper lies and deepen the wounds. The Bible teaches us that "where two or three gather in my name, there am I with them" (Matthew 18:20). This community of believers is essential in providing strength, encouragement, and accountability during and after deliverance.

For those seeking freedom, I encourage you not to walk this journey alone. Surround yourself with people who will lift you up in prayer, who will stand by you through the darkest moments, and who will remind you of your worth in Christ.

The Call to Ministers of Deliverance

To those who feel called to this ministry, I offer this word of encouragement: it is a calling of great responsibility, but also one of incredible reward. There will be challenges—times when the enemy pushes back with fury, when your faith will be tested, and when you may feel inadequate for the task at hand. But remember that it is not you who holds the power; it is Christ within you. And He has already won the battle.

In all things, be humble, be discerning, and be patient. Trust that God will equip you with what you need for every situation, and know that you are not alone in this fight. Deliverance ministry is a partnership with the Holy Spirit—allow Him to lead, and He will guide you into all truth.

A Final Word

As we conclude this journey through the realities of spiritual warfare and deliverance, I leave you with this reminder: freedom is available to all who seek it. No matter how deep the darkness may seem, no matter how long the enemy has had a foothold, God's light is stronger. The journey to deliverance may be difficult, but it is worth it, for it leads to the ultimate freedom found only in Christ.

To those who have been touched by these stories, whether you are seeking deliverance yourself or feel called to help others, know that God is with you. He is a God of redemption, healing, and hope. And He offers that same hope to each and every one of us.

In the name of Jesus, we have the victory.

Amen.

A Disobedient Group

The verses below are so important in spiritual warfare but are completely ignored in the church. My ministry is the forgotten ministry and even shunned by some circles where I have been asked to leave churches that find out about my ministry. Yet the Great Commission states that casting out demons will be a sign that accompany those who believe.

Staring into the darkness

1. Mark 16:17

"And these signs will accompany those who believe: In my name, they will drive out demons; they will speak in new tongues."

- This verse is part of the Great Commission, where Jesus tells His followers that casting out demons is one of the signs that will accompany those who believe in Him.

2. Matthew 10:1

"Jesus called his twelve disciples to him and gave them authority to drive out impure spirits and to heal every disease and sickness."

- Jesus specifically empowers His disciples with the authority to cast out unclean spirits.

3. Matthew 10:7-8

"As you go, proclaim this message: 'The kingdom of heaven has come near.' Heal the sick, raise the dead, cleanse those who have leprosy, drive out demons. Freely you have received; freely give."

- Jesus instructs His disciples to cast out demons as part of their mission to proclaim the Kingdom of Heaven.

4. Luke 9:1-2

"When Jesus had called the Twelve together, he gave them power and authority to drive out all demons and to cure diseases, and he sent them out to proclaim the kingdom of God and to heal the sick."

- Again, Jesus gives His disciples authority over all demons as part of their ministry.

5. Luke 10:17-19

"The seventy-two returned with joy and said, 'Lord, even the demons submit to us in your name.' He replied, 'I saw Satan fall like lightning from heaven. I have given you authority to trample on snakes and scorpions and to overcome all the power of the enemy; nothing will harm you.'"

- The seventy-two disciples Jesus sent out report back that they were able to cast out demons in His name, and Jesus affirms their authority over the enemy.

6. Matthew 12:28

"But if it is by the Spirit of God that I drive out demons, then the kingdom of God has come upon you."

- Jesus is speaking about casting out demons by the power of the Holy Spirit, indicating that this act is a demonstration of God's Kingdom.

7. Mark 6:7, 12-13

"Calling the Twelve to him, he began to send them out two by two and gave them authority over impure spirits... They went out and preached that people should repent. They drove out many demons and anointed many sick people with oil and healed them."

- This passage recounts Jesus sending out His disciples with authority over unclean spirits, and they exercised that authority by casting out demons.

8. Acts 8:6-7

"When the crowds heard Philip and saw the signs he performed, they all paid close attention to what he said. For with shrieks, impure spirits came out of many, and many who were paralyzed or lame were healed."

- Philip, one of the early Christians, cast out impure spirits as part of his ministry.

9. Acts 16:16-18

"Once when we were going to the place of prayer, we were met by a female slave who had a spirit by which she predicted the future. She earned a great deal of money for her owners by fortune-telling. She followed Paul and the rest of us, shouting, 'These men are servants of the Most High God, who are telling you the way to be saved.' She kept this up for many days. Finally, Paul became so annoyed that he turned around and said to the spirit, 'In the name of Jesus Christ I command you to come out of her!' At that moment the spirit left her."

- Paul casts out a spirit from a girl, demonstrating his authority in Jesus' name.

10. Acts 19:11-12

"God did extraordinary miracles through Paul, so that even handkerchiefs and aprons that had touched him were taken to the sick, and their illnesses were cured and the evil spirits left them."

- This passage highlights that even indirectly, through items touched by Paul, demons were cast out, showing the power of God's Spirit working through believers.

11. James 4:7

"Submit yourselves, then, to God. Resist the devil, and he will flee from you."

- While not directly about casting out demons, this verse emphasizes the authority believers have to resist demonic forces, which aligns with the broader biblical context of spiritual authority.

12. Ephesians 6:11-12

"Put on the full armor of God, so that you can take your stand against the devil's schemes. For our struggle is not against flesh and blood, but against the rulers, against the authorities, against the powers of this dark world and against the spiritual forces of evil in the heavenly realms."

- This passage speaks to the spiritual warfare believers are engaged in, which includes combating evil spirits.

Conclusion

These passages collectively affirm that casting out demons is a ministry that Jesus empowered His followers to carry out. They show that believers are called to exercise authority over demonic forces through the name of Jesus Christ. This mandate is an essential aspect of the broader Christian mission to proclaim the Kingdom of God and bring freedom to those oppressed by the enemy.

If anyone is interested in learning more about spiritual warfare, please feel free to connect with me on LinkedIn or by email at [your email address]. If your church would like me to give a talk on Spiritual Warfare and taking back control where you live, please contact me anytime.

Walk with God, and may the Lord Jesus Christ watch over and protect you with His loving Holy Spirit who lives within each child of God. May the peace of God be with you and in you as you continue your walk in Christ.

Love,

Russ